Shaftesbury Road, Cambridge CB2 8EA, United Kingdom

One Liberty Plaza, 20th Floor, New York, NY 10006, USA

477 Williamstown Road, Port Melbourne, VIC 3207, Australia

314–321, 3rd Floor, Plot 3, Splendor Forum, Jasola District Centre,
New Delhi – 110025, India

103 Penang Road, #05–06/07, Visioncrest Commercial, Singapore 238467

Cambridge University Press is part of Cambridge University Press & Assessment,
a department of the University of Cambridge.

We share the University's mission to contribute to society through the pursuit of
education, learning and research at the highest international levels of excellence.

www.cambridge.org
Information on this title: www.cambridge.org/9781009539364

DOI: 10.1017/9781009377720

First published 2024

A catalogue record for this publication is available from the British Library.

ISBN 978-1-009-53936-4 Hardback
ISBN 978-1-009-37771-3 Paperback
ISSN 2755-1202 (online)
ISSN 2755-1199 (print)

Cambridge Elements

Elements in Critical Issues in Teacher Education
edited by
Tony Loughland
University of New South Wales
Andy Gao
University of New South Wales
Hoa T. M. Nguyen
University of New South Wales

LANGUAGE TEACHERS' SOCIAL COGNITION

Hao Xu
Beijing Foreign Studies University

CAMBRIDGE
UNIVERSITY PRESS

Language Teachers' Social Cognition

Elements in Critical Issues in Teacher Education

DOI: 10.1017/9781009377720
First published online: June 2024

Hao Xu
Beijing Foreign Studies University
Author for correspondence: Hao Xu, xuhaokent@bfsu.edu.cn

Abstract: This Element aims to elucidate the theories of social cognition and to delineate their implications for the professional development of language teachers in primary and secondary schools. The Element first explores the concept of social cognition. The three key dimensions, that is, representation of social reality, social cognitive processing, and social mental abilities, of the social cognition theories are further elaborated with examples closely associated with language teaching and teacher development. The Element continues with more specific issues such as impression, attitude, emotion, and self-efficacy, which arise and develop as language teachers code, store, and retrieve information from social situations. The Element then discusses how social cognition influences teacher learning and development as observed and promoted within different social realities, and it ends with a call for a social-cognitive perspective on understanding language teachers' learning and development situated in diverse and changing contexts in and out of schools.

Keywords: Teacher cognition, social psychology, language teacher, teacher education, language education

ISBNs: 9781009539364 (HB), 9781009377713 (PB), 9781009377720 (OC)
ISSNs: 2755-1202 (online), 2755-1199 (print)

Contents

1 Introduction

Imagine you are Anna, who is conducting a teacher training workshop in which she introduces an innovative educational technology that she believes will enhance student engagement and learning outcomes. However, she quickly notices that some of the teacher trainees seem resistant to adopting this new tool. Initially, Anna is puzzled by their reluctance, as she sees the technology as having clear potential benefits. However, instead of simply dismissing their concerns or forcing the issue, she decides to take a social cognitive approach to understanding their resistance. She starts by engaging the teacher trainees in open dialogue, asking them to share their thoughts and concerns about the new technology. Through this process, Anna learns that the trainees are worried about how the technology will fit into their existing teaching practices, how it might impact their relationships with students, and whether it aligns with their personal values as educators. By approaching the issue from a social cognitive perspective, Anna recognises that the resistance is not simply a reaction to the technology itself but rather to its perceived social value within the educational context. She understands that the trainees are evaluating the technology according to how well it aligns with their beliefs about effective teaching and learning.

Armed with this insight, Anna adjusts her approach. She provides more opportunities for the trainees to explore and experiment with the technology in a safe and supportive environment. She also facilitates discussions about the potential benefits and challenges of integrating the tool into their teaching practices, encouraging critical reflection and collaborative problem-solving. Through this process, Anna is able to overcome the initial resistance and help the trainees embrace the new technology as a valuable addition to their teaching toolbox. By understanding their concerns from a social cognitive perspective, she is able to create a more inclusive and supportive learning environment where all voices are heard and valued.

This hypothetical example highlights the potential and value of the social cognitive approach for language teachers' cognition. By considering the social cognitive factors that influence teachers' beliefs and practices, educators can create more effective learning environments that are responsive to teachers' needs and concerns. The social cognitive approach emphasises the importance of understanding teachers' perspectives, fostering critical reflection, and facilitating collaborative problem-solving, which are crucial for the promotion of positive change and professional growth in education.

In this Element, we focus on language teachers' social cognition, a subtype of teacher cognition. The evolution of the study of language teacher cognition has been marked by distinct shifts in perspective, with increasing attention being paid to the sociocultural dimensions of teaching and learning. Initially, cognition was viewed as a component of humanity involving the individual teacher's beliefs, knowledge, and skills. However, this approach was criticised for its isolationist tendency; it failed to recognise the dynamic and interactive nature of cognition in social contexts. Subsequently, cognition came to be seen as a process of construction, with an emphasis on the role of social interactions and experiences in shaping teachers' understanding and practices. More recently, the ecological perspective has emerged, which views cognition as a reality embedded within a complex network of social, cultural, and institutional factors. This approach recognises the interconnectedness between teachers' cognitive processes and their immediate environments, highlighting the need to consider the broader ecological context. Through these shifts in perspective, the field has moved towards a more comprehensive and integrated understanding of the evolution of language teachers' cognition by acknowledging its inherently social and cultural nature.

The term 'social cognition', more specifically, refers to the ways in which individuals process, interpret, and remember information about themselves and others within a social context (Hunt et al., 2012). This concept is particularly relevant in teacher education as it sheds light on how teachers perceive and interact with their students, colleagues, and the broader educational environment. The significance of social cognition lies in its influence on teachers' beliefs, attitudes, and practices, which in turn impact student learning and development. Understanding teachers' social cognitive processes allows educators to design more effective teacher education programmes that address teachers' needs and challenges. For instance, teacher education programmes can incorporate activities that foster critical reflection and collaborative problem-solving, enabling teachers to examine their own beliefs and practices and learn from the experiences of others. Such programmes can also help teachers develop a deeper understanding of the social and cultural factors that shape learning, leading to more inclusive and responsive teaching practices.

Looking ahead, the prospects for teacher education research on social cognition are promising. More studies may explore how social cognitive factors influence teachers' professional growth and retention and how they can be leveraged to promote positive change in educational settings. Additionally, research may examine the intersection of social cognition with other areas of teacher education, such as teacher identity formation, classroom management, and the integration of technology into teaching and learning. By continuing to investigate the role of social cognition in teacher education, researchers and practitioners alike can contribute to the advancement of more effective and equitable teaching practices on a global scale.

It is important to note that social cognition is distinct from constructs such as teachers' social emotional intelligence, although both share some overlapping concepts. Social cognition, as a construct, primarily focuses on how teachers perceive, interpret, and respond to social cues and interactions within their educational context. It encompasses the cognitive processes involved in understanding others' behaviours, emotions, and intentions, as well as the ability to regulate one's own social behaviour. On the other hand, the term 'social emotional intelligence' refers to teachers' ability to effectively manage their emotions, empathise with others, and establish positive relationships in social settings (CASEL, 2003; CASEL, 2012). While both constructs are crucial for understanding teachers' professional growth and effectiveness, social cognition emphasises the cognitive aspects of social interactions, whereas social emotional intelligence emphasises the emotional and relational dimensions. By clarifying these distinctions, researchers can gain a more accurate understanding of the unique contributions of the social cognition construct to teachers' education and practice.

This Element consists of six sections, including this introduction and a concluding section. Section 2 examines the essential aspects of social cognition, exploring its definition, representations, and formation. We begin by defining social cognition, tracing its origins, and highlighting its development as a concept. We find that social cognition involves internal representations of social phenomena and cognitive processes that interpret and respond to social cues. Next, we explore various representations of social cognition, including impressions, attitudes, emotions, and self-efficacy. These elements influence how individuals perceive themselves and others, thus guiding their social behaviour and interactions. Finally, we discuss the formation and transformation of social cognition. This process involves both implicit and explicit cognitive processes that interact to shape individuals' understanding of social situations. By understanding these processes, we can gain insights into how social cognition develops and evolves over time.

In Section 3, we inquire into the various ways in which social cognition is explored, focusing on mental representations of social reality, the processing of social information, and the abilities of the social mind. By understanding these methods, we can gain deeper insights into how individuals perceive, interpret, and respond to the social world around them. First, we examine mental representations of social reality. This involves categorising and contextualising these representations to understand how individuals mentally organise and make sense of social phenomena. Categorisation helps us classify social information into meaningful groups, while contextualisation considers the broader social and cultural factors that shape these representations. Next, we investigate the processing of social information by exploring the factors that influence how individuals process social cues and the changes that occur as a result of this processing. Through understanding these processes, we can gain insights into how social information is interpreted and how it shapes individuals' responses to social situations. Finally, we unravel the abilities of the social mind. This involves reflecting on our own social cognitive processes, cultivating mindfulness to concentrate on social interactions, and developing self-efficacy to persevere when navigating social challenges. These abilities are crucial for effective social cognition and can be enhanced through various practices and interventions. By exploring these abilities, we can better understand how individuals improve their social cognitive skills and become more adept at navigating the social world.

Section 4 provides a focused exploration of language teachers' social cognitive processes, analysing how their understandings of teaching shape both their classroom practices and their personal growth as educators. The section begins by considering language teachers' views and perspectives on teaching, exploring the beliefs and values that inform their approach to instruction. It then delves into teachers' cognitive processes in relation to teaching, revealing the cognitive frameworks that underlie their decision-making. Finally, the section examines the role of social cognition in teacher development, discussing how it contributes to the acquisition of knowledge and competence as well as the emotional growth necessary for effective teaching. Through this analysis, the section aims to enhance understanding of language teachers' complex cognitive landscape and its impact on their professional lives.

Section 5, the penultimate section, explores the intricate relationship between social cognition and the professional development of language teachers. It delves into the knowledge and competence required for effective teaching, offering suggestions for future research and outlining practical applications in teacher education. The section also examines the role of motivation and emotion in teacher development, discussing how these factors influence teachers' growth and highlighting areas for further study and improvement in educational settings. Additionally, the section considers the concepts of resistance and resilience in teachers' careers, exploring how they navigate challenges and maintain their commitment to teaching. Through this comprehensive analysis, Section 5 aims to enhance understanding of the complex social cognitive process of language teacher development and to provide practical guidance for educators seeking to foster their own growth and that of their colleagues.

To summarise, this introduction has introduced the concept of social cognition and its relevance to language teachers, outlining the key themes and arguments that will be explored in depth in the subsequent sections.

Innovative exploration of language teachers' social cognition has immense significance in the field of education. This endeavour not only uncovers the intricate dynamics involved in language teachers' perception and interpretation of social interactions within the classroom but also sheds light on how their cognitive processes and beliefs shape their teaching practices. By understanding teachers' social cognition, we can gain valuable insights into the subtle nuances of classroom interactions, which ultimately impact student learning and development. This innovative approach paves the way for more effective teacher training and professional development programmes that are grounded in the realities of the classroom, thereby enhancing the quality of language education and fostering a more inclusive and equitable learning environment for all.

2 What is Social Cognition?

2.1 Defining Social Cognition

Social cognition has long been a critical component of psychological research, particularly in the field of social psychology. However, the concept remains somewhat nebulous, with many definitions and iterations of the concept present in the literature. In this section, we will delve into the origin and development of social cognition as a concept, exploring how it has evolved and developed over time. We will also examine social cognition as a mental representation, how this relates to cognitive processing, and how these two approaches interface.

2.1.1 The Origin and Development of the Concept

When approaching a new or unfamiliar concept (as 'social cognition' may be for the reader), it is helpful to have a clear understanding of its meaning and origin. Two primary approaches can be taken to gain such an understanding. The first approach is to trace the concept back to the earliest studies that mention it. This involves identifying the seminal articles or research studies that first introduced or focused on the concept. By tracing the development of the concept through its various iterations and applications, a clearer picture can be formed of how the concept has evolved and how it fits into the larger body of knowledge. This approach is particularly useful when exploring a concept that is relatively new or has undergone significant changes since its inception, which is precisely the case for social cognition. The second approach is to analyse the keywords associated with the concept. This involves a linguistic analysis of the term and its related terminology, exploring the different meanings and usages of each word. By breaking down the concept into its component parts and exploring how they relate to one another, it becomes easier to comprehend the overall meaning and significance of the concept. This approach is particularly useful when the concept is complex or multifaceted, containing numerous sub-concepts and dimensions, which is also a characteristic of the concept of social cognition. In this section, we will take both of these approaches to gain a more comprehensive understanding of social cognition as a new or unfamiliar concept, including its origins, components, and applications.

As early as the 1920s, psychologists began to shift their focus from the study of individuals in isolation to the examination of how people interact with each other within social contexts. This recognition that humans are not passive objects shaped solely by environmental contingencies but rather active agents who engage in social interaction and influence their surroundings marked a significant turning point in the field of psychology. In the decades that followed, psychologists made a sustained effort to refine and expand our understanding of social behaviour. This period was marked by theoretical advancements and empirical research that laid the groundwork for the development of Social Cognitive Theory (SCT), which was formalised in the 1980s by psychologists such as Albert Bandura as an extension of earlier social learning theory (Bandura, 1989, 1997). The core components of SCT include cognitive appraisals, self-regulatory processes, and social interactions. Social Cognitive Theory posits that individuals engage in self-regulatory processes, such as goal-setting and self-monitoring, to manage their social environments and promote adaptive outcomes (Bandura, 1989).

Social cognition as a concept originates from this larger field of research into human behaviour and social interactions. The concept emerged following a shift in focus from environmental contingencies to the examination of human agency, particularly with regard to people's active processing of social information and their intention to shape and change their social environment. Social cognition is concerned primarily with cognitive processes, such as social perception, social reasoning, and social memory, rather than with the social practices and cultural norms that are often associated with traditional sociological inquiry (Giddens et al., 2021). This emphasis on cognition reflects the underlying premise that social phenomena, like other psychological phenomena, can be understood as the product of individual cognitive processes. As such, social cognition is a psychological construct that is concerned with the ways in which individuals think about and make sense of social situations and interact with others, as well as the influence of social factors on these cognitive processes.

Given this background, we may now turn our attention to a conceptual analysis of social cognition. 'Social cognition' refers to the cognitive processes involved in understanding, interpreting, and reasoning about social information and social behaviour (Hunt et al., 2012). The term 'social' emphasises the social context and social nature of these cognitive processes, as opposed to cognitive processes that occur in isolation. The term 'cognition' refers to the mental activities that take place during information processing, including perception, attention, memory, reasoning, and decision-making (Coon et al., 2021). Social cognition combines these two domains to reflect how individuals actively process and make sense of social information while also engaging in social behaviour within a social context. It involves both self-directed cognitive processes, such as self-reflection and self-regulation, as well as processes directed towards others, such as social perception, social comparison, and social inference. Understanding these cognitive processes and their role in social behaviour is fundamental to social psychology and related fields.

2.1.2 Social Cognition as Mental Representation

Social cognition, being a psychological construct, can be approached from two major perspectives: the mental representation approach and the cognitive processing approach. The mental representation approach focuses on how people represent social information in their minds (Kempson, 1990), while the cognitive processing approach is concerned with how people process and use this information (McBride & Cutting, 2018).

'Mental representation' refers to the ways in which people encode, organise, and retrieve information in their minds (Kempson, 1990). This information can be based on individuals' past experiences, their memories, and the social information that they encounter in their daily lives. Mental representation is a critical component of social cognition because it shapes how individuals interpret, understand, and predict social behaviour.

Mental representations can take many forms, including images, symbols, concepts, and mental models (Moscovici, 2000). For example, when a student thinks about their English teacher, they may have a mental image of her or his face or a collection of memories related to the teacher. These mental representations serve as a framework for the processing and interpretation of social information. For example, if the student knows the teacher to be friendly and easy-going, this information will be processed and interpreted within the framework to shape the student's expectations and behaviour in relation to the teacher both in and out of the classroom. If the teacher provides feedback or comments on the student's work, the student will process and interpret these communications within the framework to understand their meaning and significance in terms of the student's English learning. If the student knows the teacher to be popular or respected among students, this information will be processed and interpreted within the framework to shape the student's view of the teacher's leadership or teaching style. As these examples show, mental representations help individuals make sense of complex social situations and guide their behaviour in response to those situations.

In summary, the mental representation approach is a way of understanding how individuals process and interpret social information that is related to their experiences and encounters. It emphasises the role of past experiences, memories, and social information in shaping how people think, feel, and behave in social situations. The approach assumes that people encode, organise, and retrieve social information in their minds as mental representations, which serve as frameworks guiding their social cognition and behaviour.

2.1.3 Social Cognition as Cognitive Processing

Whilst the mental representation approach is useful for understanding how people process and interpret social information in complex and dynamic social environments, it does not account for all aspects of social cognition, particularly those related to conscious, intuitive, and even automatic processes such as emotional responses and decision-making. Therefore, it is necessary to consider a second approach, which is known as 'cognitive processing'.

The cognitive processing approach views social cognition as a process of actively encoding, storing, retrieving, and using social information. It emphasises the cognitive processes involved in these activities, such as attention, memory encoding and retrieval, decision-making, and problem-solving (Frith & Blakemore, 2006). The cognitive processing approach is concerned with how individuals use their past experiences and the social information they have gathered to guide their behaviour in social situations.

This approach assumes that people encode, store, and retrieve social information using cognitive processes that are mostly subject to conscious control and manipulation. It also assumes that individual's cognitive biases and heuristics influence how they process and use social information in social situations (Priest, 2019). The cognitive processing approach thus emphasises how individuals consciously and agentically search, select, and interpret social information using their past experiences and knowledge to guide their behaviour.

For example, when a person encounters a conflict situation in a social environment, they may seek to understand it by using their past experiences and knowledge to actively search for information that is relevant to the conflict (Randolph, 2016). They may also use their past experiences to select the information that is most important and relevant to the conflict and use it to guide their behaviour in the conflict situation. It should be noted, however, that the individual's use of their past experiences and knowledge to both understand the conflict and guide their behaviour in response to it may be conducted in a biased manner that is consistent with their own values, beliefs, and interests (Eberhardt, 2020). This is one of the most prominent features of the cognitive processing that is embedded in or enabled by people's social cognition and distinguishes it from the cognitive processing that takes place within other domains.

It is evident that combining the cognitive processing approach and the mental representation approach provides a more comprehensive understanding of social cognition than applying either approach in isolation. Together, the two approaches help psychologists understand how people represent and process social information, which in turn affects how they behave and interact with others in social situations.

2.2 Representations of Social Cognition

This sub-section explores representations of social cognition, focusing on four in particular: attitude, emotion, impression, and self-efficacy. Although there are numerous types of representation, they all share a common denominator: they reflect individuals' mental realities or subjective experiences in response to external stimuli and social information.

The four representations selected for discussion in this sub-section each contribute in different ways to how people process social information. An impression is an initial evaluation or judgment of an object, person, or group, based primarily on fragmentary information and our initial feelings (Haselton & Funder, 2006). An attitude, which is a personal evaluation or judgment of an object, person, or group, is a stable and long-lasting cognitive process that evaluates behaviours and classifies them based on observed regularities (Maio et al., 2018). Emotion, on the other hand, is a fleeting and momentary response to external stimuli that often dictates our behaviour in a given situation (Niedenthal & Ric, 2017). Finally, self-efficacy is one's belief in one's ability to successfully execute a task or achieve a goal (Bandura, 1997). This sub-section will delve into each of these representations in detail, exploring their role in social cognition and how they shape our interactions with others.

2.2.1 Impression

An impression can be defined as the cognitive outcome or result of our attempt to make sense of incoming stimuli and assign meaning to them based on our past experiences and knowledge (Haselton & Funder, 2006). It involves the evaluation and categorisation of a person, object, or situation and can often lead to snap judgments and initial impressions that shape our responses and behaviours (Fletcher-Watson et al., 2008). Impressions are influenced by many factors, including our personal biases, cultural background, and social experiences, and can either be accurate or inaccurate, depending on the accuracy of our evaluation and the amount of information we have at our disposal (Ambady et al., 2000).

In this sub-section, we will explore two important concepts related to impression: personal impression and impression formation. A personal impression is one's overall evaluation and judgment of another individual (Carlston & Skowronski, 2005). It involves the cognitive process, as we navigate our social environments, of assigning meaning and value to other people based on their observable characteristics, behaviours, and traits. For instance, when we meet a new student for the first time, we quickly form an initial impression of her or his personality, appearance, and demeanour, whether or not such an impression accurately reflects what she or he is truly like. This impression may influence how we interact with and respond to that student in the future. Understanding how personal impressions are formed and the role they play in social interactions, particularly in instructional settings, is crucial to enhancing our social skills and interpersonal relationships as teachers. Impression formation, on the other hand, is the process of creating an overall picture or opinion about something or someone based on limited information or experiences (Demarais & White, 2005). It involves the cognitive process of integrating fragmented information into a meaningful whole. When we encounter new people or situations, we quickly try to make sense of them by assigning meaning to them and evaluating them based on our internal criteria and values. As mentioned earlier, the process of impression formation is influenced by many factors, including our personal biases, cultural backgrounds, and social experiences.

In their study on the role of personal perception in judgments of truthfulness in public appeals, Canter et al. (2016) argue that although many studies have been conducted on the accuracy rate of lie detection, the aspects of personal perception that underlie these judgments are not well understood. To explore this subject, the researchers measured thirty academics' personal perceptions and truthfulness judgments of people making televised appeals. Twelve different appeals were used; six were genuine and six were false. The researchers also used a 14-item scale to measure personal perception, which included both global, abstract judgments (open, deceptive, genuine, trustworthy, and emotional) and behavioural indices (such as facial pleasantness, tension, and vocal certainty). Multiple regression analysis indicated that personal perceptions of openness, (non)deceptiveness, genuineness, trustworthiness, and verbal plausibility were significant predictors of truthfulness judgments. The researchers thus suggest that future research should further explore the relationship between personal perceptions as components of truth judgments and accuracy, which may have vast implications for our social practices. Understanding how we form impressions and judgments about others is crucial for effectively communicating, building trust, and maintaining healthy relationships. A better understanding of the cognitive processes involved in personal perception can help us evaluate their accuracy and objectivity and make more informed decisions in our social interactions. As detailed in the aforementioned study (Canter et al., 2016), when dealing with law enforcement or legal systems, accurate assessments of witness testimony or defendant demeanour require an understanding of the cognitive processes involved in the formation of impressions. Similarly, the ability to read your students' cues and understand their emotions and goals can be equally essential for effective teaching and classroom management.

All impressions, including personal perception, are formed by certain cognitive processes, which means that impression formation is a central issue in studies of impression. For instance, Sutherland et al. (2017) examine the formation of facial first impressions, focusing on how social judgements are influenced by both changeable and invariant facial properties. They found that people's first impressions of faces in photos can depend just as much on the temporary features of the photo image as on the consistent features of the face itself. In other words, there are two influences on our first impressions of faces in photos: the temporary features of the photo image – this could be something like how bright or dark the photo is, or how clear or blurry it is – and the consistent features of the face itself, which could be things like the shape of the face, the size of the nose, or the expression on the face. This is to say that when forming first impressions of faces in photos, people tend to pay roughly equal amounts of attention to these two influences. Clearly, studies on impression formation are important because they help us understand how we form impressions and make judgments about others. This is a crucial element of all our social interactions, including classroom-based language teaching, because our impressions of others and how those impressions are formed influence how we interact with other people, whether in business, educational, personal, or other social contexts.

2.2.2 Attitude

As previously discussed, an impression is a somewhat fleeting and momentary evaluation or judgment of an object, person, or group, often based on fragmentary information and our initial feelings. Unlike an impression, an attitude is a more stable and long-lasting evaluation or judgment of an object, person, or group (Maio et al., 2018). The term usually refers to a person's overall evaluation of a certain thing or person and includes both positive and negative evaluations. For example, a person may have a positive attitude towards a particular teacher, believing that her or his teaching is inspiring and effective, while another person may have a negative attitude towards the same teacher, believing that she or he neglects to provide individual feedback to students who need it. The attitudes people assume tend to last longer than impressions, and thus influence our social cognition and behaviour in a more enduring manner. Therefore, attitude and impression are two different cognitive processes in social cognition: an attitude is more stable and long-lasting, while an impression is more fleeting and momentary.

Attitudes are individuals' attempts to account for observed regularities (King, 2022). Naturally, these regularities can and should be classified and evaluated. There are thus two main types of attitudes: attitudes that classify behaviours and attitudes that evaluate behaviours. Attitudes that classify behaviours are concerned with sorting or categorising behaviours into groups or classes based on observable characteristics or patterns. These classifications are based on the behaviours themselves, not necessarily on the observer's personal feelings or beliefs about the behaviour. For example, a language student may have an attitude that classifies different types of teaching activities into modalities like listening, speaking, reading, and writing. Another student may classify their teacher's behaviours when implementing these activities according to the different aspects of linguistic knowledge to be taught, such as pronunciation, vocabulary, and grammar, instead of the modalities of these activities. As the same social behaviours are classified in different ways, they are understood in different ways, and thus differences in attitude may arise.

Attitudes that evaluate behaviours, on the other hand, are concerned with judgments or evaluations of a behaviour itself, independent of any classification system. These evaluations often concern the behaviour's value, importance, desirability, or acceptability to the observer (Cooper et al., 2015). Consider a language learner who holds the attitude that language practice such as speaking or writing is crucial for improving their skills, and explanations of grammar or vocabulary are less important. This evaluative attitude would undoubtedly influence how she or he responds to or reacts to certain learning behaviours encouraged or required by her or his teacher in the classroom, as well as the learning strategies she or he employs.

Understanding the classification and evaluation of behaviours that people's attitudes reflect is crucial for understanding their beliefs and values, because it can reveal how individuals perceive the world around them and what they find important. In real research practice, however, researchers tend to examine both the classification and evaluation of behaviours in attitude studies. For instance, in an attempt to identify differences in consumer attitudes towards local foods in organic and national voluntary quality certification schemes, Hristov et al. (2023) compared consumer attitudes towards organic food and local food produced under a national quality scheme, aiming to gain insights into the issue of consumer segmentation in terms of trust towards organic and local food, along with socioeconomic characteristics and other important factors in this complex interaction. The study focused on consumers' attitudes and beliefs in relation to two quality schemes for special Slovenian foods: one for foods produced using 'organic' methods and one for foods of 'selected quality'. The research concentrated on two groups of consumers who had a high level of trust in these two quality schemes. Comparative analysis was carried out to detect potential differences between the consumer segments in terms of their socio-demographic profiles, understanding of the definition of local food, attitudes towards local food, trust in food producers and institutions, and willingness to buy local food. The results showed that both consumer groups had a similar understanding of local food, and that region-based interpretations were more important than country-based ones. The 'organic' group was more international and supportive of the local community, regardless of geographical distance, than the 'selected quality' group. This shows that when people are classified according to their attitudes towards certain social realities, the evaluations they make may be better observed and compared. This study emphasises the value of studying attitudes holistically rather than separately, as both classification and evaluation provide important insights into people's beliefs and values.

2.2.3 Emotion

The concept of emotion is closely related to that of attitude, as attitude can be seen as a form of emotional response to external stimuli in society. However, emotion extends beyond attitude and involves a more immediate and intuitive process, which is often triggered by external environmental cues rather than cognitive processing (Niedenthal & Ric, 2017). In this sub-section, we focus on emotions that are evoked or modulated by social issues rather than those that arise solely from an individual's physical movement or physiological state.

Emotions can be classified into primary or secondary emotions (Damasio, 1994): primary emotions include happiness, anger, sadness, surprise, fear, and disgust, which are innate and universal across cultures; secondary emotions are more situation-specific and modulated by our life experiences, beliefs, cultural backgrounds, and other contextual factors. These emotions often arise from complex cognitive processes and may not be experienced as physiological sensations. Emotions serve important functions in social cognition. They help us quickly respond to environmental challenges and threats and mobilise our resources to deal with these situations; emotions also help us quickly evaluate other people's actions and intentions and respond appropriately, and thus play a critical role in social interaction (Lench, 2018).

Researchers have studied emotion from multiple perspectives, focusing for example on examining emotional traits or emotional labour. An individual's emotional traits are their characteristic patterns of emotional experience and response, which tend to remain stable across time and situations (Hinshelwood, 2023). Emotional labour, meanwhile, is the process of managing one's emotions and expressions to meet the demands of a job or social interaction (Wharton, 2009). Emotional traits and emotional labour are particularly important and inspiring aspects of research on emotion. Studying emotional traits allows researchers to understand how individuals' characteristic patterns of emotional experience and response shape their behaviour and interactions with others. For example, a language learner who is generally not anxious may respond calmly and confidently to stressful situations such as exams or public speaking, while a learner who is highly anxious may respond to such situations with heightened levels of uneasiness and worry. Understanding the role of emotional traits in determining how people feel and behave in different situations can help us develop interventions that target individuals' characteristic emotional patterns. Emotional labour research, on the other hand, has shed light on the cognitive, physiological, and expressive processes that people engage in to manage their emotions and expressions in response to social or work-related demands (Pugh, 2001). This research also helps us understand how emotional labour can have negative effects on individuals' mental health and well-being if the required emotional regulation is too burdensome or unrealistic (Hochschild, 2012). Understanding the processes involved in emotional labour and how they can be harmful to mental health is an important part of developing interventions that help individuals better manage their emotions in different social and work-related contexts.

Numerous studies have investigated teachers' emotional traits (e.g., Wang & Hall, 2021). A recent study used a structural equation model to analyse the role of emotional regulation, intrinsic job satisfaction, and affect in teachers' life satisfaction (Luque-Reca et al., 2022). The researchers collected data from school teachers by asking them to complete a questionnaire designed to measure their characteristic patterns of emotional response to work-related stressors. The questionnaire included items that probed into teachers' tendency to experience emotions such as anxiety, anger, and guilt in response to work-related issues. One key finding of the study was that the participating teachers' emotional traits were strongly linked to their evaluations of work-related stressors and their willingness to take action to address these stressors. For example, teachers who were highly anxious reported feeling more worried and nervous about work-related issues than less anxious teachers and were more likely to express a need to reduce their workload or seek support from colleagues or superiors. In contrast, teachers who were not anxious reported feeling relatively calm and confident when facing work-related stressors and were more likely to seek ways to improve their efficiency at work or enhance their teaching methods. Another key finding of the study was that the teachers' emotional traits were strongly linked to their evaluations of students' behaviour and their teaching effectiveness. For example, teachers who scored highly for anger reported feeling more irritated and impatient with students' behaviour and were more likely to consider transferring to a different teaching position or seeking a different career. In contrast, teachers with low scores for anger reported feeling relatively tolerant and patient when dealing with students' behaviour and were more likely to seek ways to improve their teaching methods or engage in more active learning strategies with students. This study therefore provides a good example of the importance and value of studying emotional traits in the context of work-related stressors and teaching effectiveness. The findings also imply that interventions designed to target teachers' characteristic emotional patterns may be an effective way of helping them better manage their responses, evaluations, and willingness to take action when facing work-related stressors.

Emotional traits alone do not fully capture the complexity of emotional experience and expression. We also need to consider emotional labour to reveal the full range of factors that shape individuals' emotional experiences and expressions. For instance, in a review article, Purper et al. (2023) explore the concept of emotional labour as performed by early childhood teachers and review research on teachers' experience of emotional labour in the classroom. The review seems to suggest that it is inevitable that early childhood teachers will perform emotional labour, but appropriate strategies can alleviate the job burnout associated with it. Further, the review also shows that the experience of emotional labour may vary among early childhood teachers from different backgrounds and that it is necessary to further understand differences in emotional labour among various populations to find targeted solutions. This shows that the emotional labour of early childhood teachers, like that of most other teacher groups, is a complex and important issue. More research is thus required to gain a deeper understanding of emotional labour in this context and find effective solutions.

2.2.4 Self-efficacy

Self-efficacy, as an aspect of social cognition, is distinct from the constructs of impression, attitude, and emotion that were discussed in the preceding subsections. Self-efficacy refers to an individual's belief in their ability to perform a specific task or behaviour (Bandura, 1997), rather than on external factors such as others' impressions and evaluations of oneself, or one's impressions and evaluations of others. Therefore, self-efficacy is more inward-focused than the other constructs and emphasises individuals' cognitions of themselves.

Defining self-efficacy as people's beliefs about their abilities to perform a variety of actions that can influence the direction of their lives, the theory of self-efficacy posits that individuals' beliefs about their abilities are critical determinants of their behaviour and performance (Bandura, 1997). These beliefs are individuals' convictions about their abilities to perform a variety of actions that can influence the direction their lives take (Donohoo, 2016). According to the theory of self-efficacy, they are critical determinants of behaviour and performance, affecting how individuals approach tasks, how they react to challenges and setbacks, and how they persist in the face of difficulties. The influence of one's beliefs on one's development is also significant. A person's beliefs about their abilities can either enhance or hinder their development and progress in various aspects of life. For example, a strong belief in one's ability to learn new skills or achieve personal goals can provide the motivation and perseverance needed to overcome challenges and succeed. Conversely, beliefs that limit a person's actions or prevent them from taking risks can prevent them from developing new skills or expanding their horizons. In self-efficacy research, it is thus important to examine both beliefs in themselves and their influence on human development. This can help us develop better interventions and support mechanisms to enhance individuals' self-efficacy and ultimately improve their chances of success in different domains of life.

During the COVID-19 pandemic, teachers were forced to quickly adapt their teaching methods and switch to remote learning. Vidergor (2023) aimed to understand whether teachers considered themselves innovative and how this affected their self-efficacy, sense of accountability, and teaching practices in terms of distance learning. The researcher surveyed 200 elementary and secondary school teachers in Israel and found that the teachers' self-perception of their innovativeness was significantly related to their self-efficacy, sense of accountability, and teaching practices in terms of distance learning. Additionally, it was found that there was a positive relationship between the number of years of work experience a teacher had and their self-perception of their innovativeness, with more experienced teachers rating themselves as more innovative than less experienced teachers. Professional development, on the other hand, did not affect teachers' self-perceived innovativeness but did have a positive impact on their teaching practices when conducting distance learning. Based on these findings, Vidergor (2023) suggests that it is important to focus on promoting teachers' self-perception of their innovativeness and encouraging them to create novel and tailored combinations of hybrid learning methods in remote learning settings. As the findings show, this study helps to emphasise the importance of investigating teachers' beliefs and understanding their impact on teacher development in the context of remote learning, which constitute major issues for self-efficacy research.

Another example is provided by a study that used data from 91,768 teachers in 11,523 schools across 46 countries to investigate the association between teachers' intercultural self-efficacy and their individual experiences and contexts at the school and country levels (Schwarzenthal et al., 2023). The study found that intercultural professional development, teacher mobility, and multicultural school climates were positively related to teachers' intercultural self-efficacy, but multicultural education policy at the country level was not robustly associated with teachers' intercultural self-efficacy. These findings suggest that both individual and contextual aspects should be considered when examining teachers' intercultural self-efficacy. Although the study focuses on exploring the association between teachers' intercultural self-efficacy and their individual experiences and contexts, the findings reveal that teachers' intercultural self-efficacy is positively related to intercultural professional development, teacher mobility, and multicultural school climates; these factors can all influence teachers' beliefs and development.

2.3 Formation and Transformation of Social Cognition

This sub-section focuses on the dynamic nature of social cognition – its formation and transformation – as distinct from its representations, which were examined in the previous sub-section. We specifically concentrate on the dual process model and the implicit/explicit processes that shape our social understanding. The dual process model posits that we have two different ways of thinking about and processing social information: one is a controlled and effortful way that allows us to carefully consider information and use rules to reason; the other is an automatic and effortless way that is faster but relies on patterns and guesses to a greater extent (Hunt et al., 2012). We then distinguish between implicit and explicit processing in social cognition, discussing their characteristics.

2.3.1 Dual Process Model

The dual process model, a class of various specific models, postulates that humans engage in two distinct modes of processing social information: a controlled and effortful mode that allows rule-based reasoning, and a fast and effortless mode that relies more heavily on patterns and guesses (Hunt et al., 2012), as shown in Figure 1. As Smith and DeCoster (2000) state, all dual-process models typically have three key elements: (1) they explain when and how people quickly process social information in an intuitive, effortless, and automatic way; (2) they explain how people process information more extensively when they are motivated and capable; and (3) they outline the conditions that help people switch between the two processes. The central idea presented in the dual process model is that the formation and transformation of social cognition do not happen as a single process but rather as a system of interacting cognitive processes (Amodio, 2019). The model views social cognition as a dynamic and multifaceted phenomenon that is influenced by controlled and effortful processing as well as fast and effortless processing. The model outlines the conditions that facilitate shifts between the two modes of processing, thus allowing individuals to adaptively respond to different social situations. In summary, the dual process model provides a framework for understanding the complex and dynamic nature of social cognitive processing.

The dual process model can help us understand how people form and transform their impressions and attitudes as representations of social cognition, which we outlined in the previous sub-section. In the controlled and effortful mode, individuals carefully consider information and weigh different options when making impressions or forming attitudes. For example, when forming impressions of a stranger, they may actively collect information about the person, consider their background, behaviour, and other relevant factors, and then make a judgment. In the fast and effortless mode, people often rely on heuristics or patterns to quickly form impressions or attitudes (Bluemke et al., 2010). For instance, they may use stereotypes or priming effects to quickly categorise people based on their appearance or other visible characteristics. When primed with

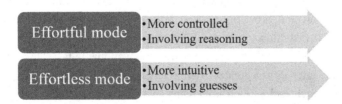

Figure 1 The dual process model of social cognitive processing.

certain information or cues, people can also quickly form attitudes that are different from their initial impressions. The dual process model can help explain why people sometimes make mistakes in impression formation or attitude change: they may rely too much on fast and effortless processing when they should engage in more effortful and controlled processing. The dual process model can also help us understand the conditions under which people engage in controlled and effortful processing rather than fast and effortless processing. In some situations, people may automatically shift between the two modes of processing based on the social context or the requirements of the task. The dual process model can help us understand how people flexibly shift between different modes of processing and adjust their impressions and attitudes accordingly.

Such social cognitive processing also takes place in language teachers' social cognition, as their attitudes and impressions are influenced by the two modes of processing in the classroom. In a controlled and effortful mode, language teachers may engage in careful consideration when forming impressions of their students. For example, they may observe their students' language proficiency, learning styles, and progress in class and also collect feedback from other teachers or students to gain a more comprehensive understanding of the students' performance and characteristics. With all this information, teachers can then make more accurate evaluations and adjust their teaching methods accordingly. On the other hand, in the fast and effortless mode, language teachers may form quick impressions of their students based on surface information or first impressions. For instance, they may judge a student as 'talented' or 'slow' based on the student's performance in a single class, ignoring other factors that may affect the student's performance. However, such quick impressions may not always be accurate and may lead to biased evaluations of students' abilities or progress. Language teachers may also need to shift between the two modes of processing in the classroom to effectively manage their teaching and respond to the different needs of their students. Teachers may shift from the fast and effortless mode to the controlled and effortful mode when they need to make more accurate evaluations or solve complex teaching problems. For example, when evaluating a student's writing skills, teachers may first quickly scan the student's work and form a first impression, but may then need to shift to a controlled and effortful mode to carefully analyse samples of the student's writing, taking into account multiple factors such as grammar, vocabulary, and content organisation.

2.3.2 Implicit and Explicit Processes

In the previous sub-section, we explored the dual processes that occur within the system of social cognition. We will now delve into the distinct characteristics of each process itself, exploring how the processes themselves can vary. Each of the two broad categories of processing in the dual process model has unique characteristics which must be further addressed.

Examining the characteristics of attitude formation as a social cognitive process, Gawronski and Bodenhausen (2006) clearly distinguish between implicit and explicit attitudes. Specifically, they define implicit attitudes or associations as affect-laden associations which are automatically activated by an internal or external stimulus. These associations are not dependent on whether people believe the association to be valid. The key contribution of Gawronski and Bodenhausen's (2006) distinction between implicit and explicit processes (as illustrated in Figure 2) is that it allows for a more nuanced understanding of the psychological mechanisms that underlie attitude formation and transformation. This distinction advances our understanding of why certain processes of social cognition are more intuitive, effortless, and automatic: the key factor is not necessarily their degree of automation, but rather how emotional factors trigger them.

Consider a professor named Dr. X, who is known for his rigorous but engaging teaching style. He is highly respected by his students for his expertise in second language acquisition theory and his ability to make dry language concepts come alive through lively classroom discussions. One day, Dr. X is leading a discussion of interlanguage and how it relates to language learners' development of language proficiency when a student named Y asks a question in English but switches to their native language midway through the sentence. This switch catches Dr. X off guard, as he has not encountered this behaviour in the classroom before. His initial reaction is one of surprise and confusion, which are emotional responses to this unexpected turn of events. At the same time, his implicit process of social cognition might kick in, causing him to make assumptions about the reasons for the student's behaviour. He might assume that the student finds their native language more comfortable or useful for expressing their ideas fully, or that they are concerned about how others in the class might react to their use of their native language. This assumption could lead Dr. X to change his teaching approach in the future to better prepare students for

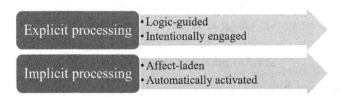

Figure 2 The contrast between explicit and implicit processing.

translanguaging situations or to create a more inclusive classroom environment that encourages students to use any language that they feel comfortable with. In conclusion, Dr. X's emotional response of surprise and confusion triggered an implicit process of social cognition, leading him to make assumptions about the student's behaviour and engage in specific classroom strategies to address the issue in the future.

Clearly, emotional factors play a crucial role in the complex processes of social cognition by acting as triggers for implicit processing (Frith & Frith, 2008), which can facilitate further processing in both controlled and effortless ways. Language teachers are not immune to these emotional triggers, and their responses to classroom situations can have profound effects on the learning experiences of their students. A thorough understanding of how emotions influence social cognition allows language teachers to gain a deeper insight into the dynamics of the classroom environment and adopt more effective teaching strategies that enhance student learning outcomes. In conclusion, emotional triggers during social cognition have the potential to facilitate further processing and inform language teachers' decision-making processes in the classroom.

3 How is Social Cognition Explored?

This section focuses on the methodological aspects of exploring and studying social cognition. It provides an overview of the methodological approaches, methods, and techniques used when researching social cognition. It also discusses how these methods have been applied to address the three major issues in social cognition research: mental representations of social reality, processing of social information, and the abilities of the social mind. Specifically, this section presents research studies that use different methods to address these three major issues in social cognition research. Each sub-section will feature a few studies that clearly illustrate how a particular method was implemented and the significant findings it produced. By showcasing actual research studies, this section aims to provide the reader with a tangible foundation for understanding how different methods have been applied to address the three major issues in social cognition research and inspire further discussion and exploration in this field.

3.1 Examining Mental Representations of Social Reality

Categorising and contextualising mental representations of social cognition is a key method of studying these representations. In this sub-section, we showcase how the categorisation and contextualisation of mental representations such as attitude and identity can better inform our understanding of social cognition.

3.1.1 Categorising Mental Representations

Mental representations can and should be categorised. For instance, attitude, which is often described as a form of mental representation in the context of social cognition, plays a crucial role in how individuals process and interpret social information. An attitude can be defined as an individual's overall evaluation or appraisal of a particular target or situation, and it can influence how that individual perceives, interprets, and reacts to that target or situation (Maio et al., 2018). Categorising attitudes is of fundamental importance for understanding their effects on social cognition and behaviour. In this sub-section, we explore methods of categorising attitudes, providing specific examples of how these methods have been used in social cognition research.

Reeves (2006) explored secondary school teachers' attitudes towards the inclusion of English-Language Learners (ELLs) in mainstream classrooms. The researcher explored four categories of teacher attitudes: views on ELLs, modifying coursework, professional development, and language and language learning. Findings from a survey of 279 high school teachers indicated neutral to slightly positive attitudes towards including ELLs in the classroom, somewhat positive attitudes towards modifying coursework, neutral attitudes towards professional development, and misconceptions about how second languages are learned.

The researcher used a specific categorisation system to organise and examine the attitudes of the teachers. She broke down the teachers' attitudes into four distinct categories that allowed for a more targeted examination of the data, as follows:

(1) Attitudes towards ELL inclusion: the extent to which teachers supported or opposed the inclusion of ELLs in their classrooms. The researcher explored their willingness to integrate ELLs into their regular classes and address their unique needs.

(2) Coursework modifications for ELLs: teachers' attitudes towards modifying coursework or curriculum for ELLs. The researcher looked at whether teachers felt it was necessary to adapt or modify course content, teaching methods, or assessment strategies to better support ELLs.

(3) Professional development for working with ELLs: teachers' attitudes towards professional development opportunities designed to enhance their ability to work effectively with ELLs. The researcher explored the teachers' level of interest and willingness to participate in workshops, trainings, or other learning experiences aimed at improving their knowledge and skills in this area.

(4) Perceptions of language and language learning: teachers' beliefs and misconceptions about how second languages are learned. The researcher

looked at whether the teachers subscribed to any common misconceptions about the language learning process or whether they had a nuanced understanding of it.

By organising her data into these four categories, the researcher was able to gain a more comprehensive understanding of the teachers' attitudes and how they related to specific aspects of ELL inclusion in their classrooms. This approach allowed the researcher to identify patterns and trends within the data, which in turn informed her conclusions and recommendations for practice.

Another example is a study by Wang et al. (2022) which delves into elementary school teachers' attitudes towards immigrant students and their families in Russia and Taiwan. Using qualitative research methods, data were collected to allow the identification of teachers' attitudes and orientations towards cultural diversity in the classroom. The attitudes of teachers were classified into three categories: attitudes towards children, parents, and diverse ethnic groups. The study found that region-specific attitudes were similar in both regions, with a particular focus on cognitive development. The findings indicated that Russian teachers might not acknowledge cultural differences in the classroom (personal attitude) and maintained high expectations for all students (professional attitude). On the other hand, Taiwanese teachers, who had prior experience of working with cultural differences, were more open to cultural diversity. The findings suggest that teachers of immigrant students often face language barriers, and some are less welcoming of immigrants in their home country. Educators make judgments about immigrants based on their country of origin, which may promote prejudice. Many teachers dislike students from social minorities, and their negative attitudes about student achievement lead to low expectations. However, some teachers are more tolerant and engage in multicultural activities in the classroom.

This study's classification of teachers' attitudes is more specific than many other studies, which use broader categorisations such as positive or negative attitudes. Instead of just categorising attitudes as positive or negative, this study looked at three specific areas: attitudes towards children, parents, and diverse ethnic groups. This approach allowed the researchers to examine teachers' attitudes towards each of these groups separately and more accurately capture their feelings and beliefs with regard to immigrant students and their families. By breaking down attitudes into these three categories, the study allowed the identification of unique patterns and trends within the data. This enabled the researchers to examine how teachers' attitudes towards immigrant children differed from their attitudes towards immigrant parents or diverse ethnic groups. This level of detail provided a more nuanced understanding of teachers' attitudes and allowed the researchers to identify specific beliefs and approaches within each category.

This shows that the importance of conceptual work and the clear categorisation of mental representations, such as attitudes towards complex issues like ELL inclusion and cultural diversity, cannot be overstated. The conceptual work, which often involves breaking a concept down into different facets or dimensions, lays the foundation for further examination and analysis. It not only refines our understanding of the concept but also informs research design. Hence, it is crucial to avoid overlaps and maintain a clear-cut categorisation. The categorisation should not only reflect our existing theoretical understanding but also align with the data gathered during a pilot study, as it did in the example study. This approach enables us to gain a more comprehensive understanding of the phenomenon under study and develop meaningful conclusions that can inform practice.

3.1.2 Contextualising Mental Representations

Categorising mental representations of social cognition is crucial, but contextualising these representations is equally important. As researchers seek to gain a more realistic understanding of how social cognition is reflected in mental representations, they must also consider the diverse contexts in which these representations emerge. Mental representations of social cognition are dynamic and can be influenced by various contextual factors. For example, individuals' ethnic and cultural backgrounds and their life experiences can shape their mental representations. Contextualising mental representations involves taking these extrinsic factors into account and understanding how they shape the content and structure of mental representations. Moreover, contextualising mental representations also involves exploring how these representations develop and change over time. Researchers must consider how past experiences, social interactions, and cultural norms shape the development of mental representations. Understanding the temporal dimension of mental representations is essential for gaining a comprehensive understanding of how individuals process and interpret social information. Contextualising mental representations is also particularly important for informing effective educational and intervention strategies. Understanding how mental representations develop and are influenced by contextual factors can help designers create more culturally sensitive educational practices that are tailored to the specific needs of students.

Xu's (2019) study investigating the impact of the promotion of Putonghua (Standard Chinese) on individuals' social interactions and language identities in multilingual minority regions in China focuses on identities. Identities are an important form of mental representation of social cognition, and the specific sociolinguistic context Xu studied is different from many other multilingual societies where various languages have equal status in law. Thus, the study's emphasis on the intersection between language proficiency, cultural background, and social environment sheds new light on how language policies and cultural background mediate individuals' access to social resources, participation in society, and a sense of identity.

Specifically, the study probed the impact of promoting Putonghua on individuals' social interactions and language identity in multilingual minority regions of China. Employing the construct of a linguistic marketplace, the study explored factors that mediate access to this market. The twenty-four research subjects, hailing from multilingual minority regions in Xinjiang, Tibet, and Inner Mongolia, exhibited different language backgrounds (being either monolingual or bilingual) and lived in societal contexts where either Putonghua or a minority language held sway. Data were collected through relatively lengthy, semi-structured interviews and observations made in the workplace. Analysis of this dataset exposed the complex interrelationships between people's language proficiency as linguistic capital, their exchange of and investment in this capital, and the formation and transformation of their identities. The study brings to light the role of Putonghua, as a high-status language, in either providing or preventing access to other forms of linguistic capital in the linguistic market, depending on an individual's proficiency in Putonghua. In other words, the study found that proficiency in Putonghua serves as a 'ticket' to the linguistic market, without which linguistic capital from other languages cannot be accessed or exchanged.

Thus, contextualising mental representations of social cognition is crucial for understanding how individuals process and interpret social information. Contextualising these representations involves exploring how cultural, historical, and societal factors shape individuals' mental representations of social cognition. By taking into account the cultural context in which mental representations are formed, we can gain a more accurate, and often more novel, understanding of how individuals' social cognition is influenced by their cultural background. Contextualising mental representations of social cognition allows us to explore how these cultural differences shape individuals' responses to social stimuli and their ability to effectively engage in social interaction.

3.2 Investigating the Processing of Social Information

Research on the processing of social cognition often involves unique challenges due to its complexity and the inherent difficulty of experimentally manipulating and observing these processes. Research on processing typically focuses on how cognitive processes shape our understanding, interpretation, and response to other people and social situations. The methodological constraints inherent to experimental research can make it difficult to fully explore and capture the intricate details of social cognition processing. As a result, research in this area typically focuses on how cognitive processing is influenced by various factors. These factors may include, but are not limited to, an individual's emotional state, personality traits, cultural background, and life experiences (Herpertz & Bertsch, 2014; Koelkebeck et al., 2017; Van Rheenen et al., 2014). Additionally, researchers also seek to understand the changes in behaviour, attitude, or social perception that result from cognitive processing. By studying these changes, researchers can gain a more comprehensive understanding of the role that cognitive processing plays in social cognition. In this sub-section, we use example studies to showcase how the processing of social cognition can be examined in terms of changes in social cognition and the factors that influence this processing.

3.2.1 Factors Influencing Social Cognition Processing

The processing of social cognition is a complex and dynamic process that can be influenced by various factors. One important factor is the emotional state of the individual, as emotions have been shown to play a critical role in social cognition (Van Rheenen et al., 2014). For instance, individuals in a positive emotional state tend to interpret social stimuli in a more positive light, while those in a negative emotional state may have a more negative bias when interpreting social information. Similarly, the cultural background of an individual can also influence social cognition processing, possibly due to differences in values, norms, and beliefs across cultures (Koelkebeck et al., 2017). For instance, individuals from collectivistic cultures may prioritise the needs of the group over those of the individual, leading to different social cognitive processes. Additionally, life experiences, such as previous interactions with others, can shape an individual's social cognitive processes. For example, someone who has had negative experiences with a particular group of people may harbour more negative stereotypes and prejudices towards that group, leading to different cognitive processes during social interactions. Finally, personality traits can also influence social cognition processing (Herpertz & Bertsch, 2014). Individuals who are highly neurotic or narcissistic, for instance, may have different social cognitive processes compared to those who do not have these traits.

In numerous empirical studies, however, it has been observed that the factors that shape the processing of social cognition can be investigated conjointly, independent of their categorical distinctions. Chen and Abdullah's (2023) study is a good example: it delves into the causes of the inconsistent implementation of equitable practices by English as a Foreign Language (EFL) teachers despite their equity-oriented mindset. Criticism has previously been levelled at these teachers for not translating their beliefs into practice, and it is important to expose the reasons for this disparity to address it. The criticism directed at these teachers for not translating their beliefs into practice underscores the fundamental issue that there is insufficient understanding of the processing of teachers' social cognition. This gap in comprehension can lead to misguided efforts to address educational disparities because it obscures the reasons behind the teachers' actions, beliefs, and practices. Addressing this lack of understanding is paramount when developing equitable and effective teaching methods.

The interpretative qualitative approach adopted in this study highlights the factors that contribute to the gap between EFL teachers' equity-oriented cognition and their practices, hence revealing the processing of teachers' cognition. The study used classroom observation and stimulated recall interviews with ten university teachers to gain an in-depth understanding of the reasons for the cognition-practice inconsistency. This approach allowed the researchers to capture the teachers' experiences and their perspectives on equitable teaching practices. The results of the study identify two experiential factors: unpleasant schooling experiences and limited effective training, as well as five contextual factors: unfavourable student-related factors, inharmonious classroom climates, toxic school contexts, equity-deficient education systems, and negative social cultures. These factors were found to mediate the relationship between teachers' equity-oriented cognition and their actual practice.

The findings of this study have implications for understanding the reasons underlying the failure of EFL teachers to implement equitable practices effectively. The researchers propose an equity-oriented teaching framework that may help to eliminate the constraining effect of these identified factors. This framework can be used as a guide for teacher training programmes and educational policymakers, helping EFL teachers close the gap between their equity-oriented cognition and their actual practice.

In summary, this study on EFL teachers effectively demonstrates the importance and benefits of researching the factors influencing social cognition for the purpose of understanding the processing of social cognition.

3.2.2 Changes Brought by the Processing

The preceding sub-section examined the factors that shape the processing of social cognition. This sub-section explores the ways in which this processing causes a range of changes in individuals' thoughts, feelings, and behaviours.

One important change is the development of more accurate social understanding. Through processing social information in a cognitive system that is biased towards noticing threatening and negative cues, individuals may be better able to comprehend the emotional and behavioural states of others, which is an essential skill for effective social communication (Keltner et al., 2013). Another change that can result from processing social cognition is the modulation of one's own emotions (Kut, 2012). When individuals process social information, they may engage in emotional self-regulation by making an effort to control their own emotional responses in order to achieve a desired emotional state or goal (Beauregard, 2004). This ability to regulate one's emotions is crucial for maintaining positive social relationships and preventing conflict or other negative outcomes. The processing of social cognition can also lead to the development of an ability to take more empathetic perspectives. This skill involves an ability to understand and appreciate others' emotions, thoughts, and viewpoints, which is important for effective conflict resolution and teamwork (Decety & Ickes, 2011). Social cognition processing can activate the neural circuits involved in affective processes and strengthen the neural connections between the self and others, enabling individuals to better understand others' emotions and perspectives. Finally, the processing of social cognition can modify the expression of prejudice and stereotypes. A prejudice is an attitude or belief that is negative or hostile towards a person or group because of their membership in a particular social category (Kite & Whitley, 2016), while a stereotype is a widely held but oversimplified belief about a person or group based on their membership in such a category (Nadler & Voyles, 2020). Social cognition processing can help individuals override these biased responses and develop more inclusive and open-minded attitudes towards others.

Changes in social cognition due to its processing occur not only in terms of intensity or quantity, but also in terms of nature – in other words, the nature of one's social cognition of a particular social reality may change. For instance, Xu's (2013) study reflects such a change in the nature of social cognition by documenting the transformation of Chinese EFL teachers' professional identities during their initial years of teaching in K-12 schools.

In social representation theory (Moscovici, 2000; Moskowitz, 2005), cognition can be classified, based on different natures of cognition, as rule-based, cue-based, exemplar-based, or schema-based. Rule-based cognition is an individual's ability to apply specific rules or algorithms to problem-solving situations. This type of cognition is characterised by logical and systematic thinking, allowing individuals to quickly process information and make decisions. Rule-based cognition is typically favoured in situations where quick and accurate decisions are necessary, such as math or science problems. Cue-based cognition, on the other hand, involves the ability to attend to and process specific environmental cues or features. For example, a person with cue-based cognition may use visual or auditory clues to determine how they should react to a given situation. This type of cognition involves paying attention to external stimuli, thus allowing individuals to respond appropriately to their environment. Exemplar-based cognition is the ability to use past examples or 'exemplars' as a guide for decision-making or problem-solving. This type of cognition allows individuals to compare new situations to those they have encountered in the past, using the knowledge gained from these past experiences to inform their current actions. Exemplar-based cognition is particularly useful when making decisions that require different options to be weighed based on their similarity to known examples. Finally, schema-based cognition is the ability to organise information into meaningful patterns or 'schemas' that can be applied to different situations. This type of cognition involves using existing knowledge structures or 'schemas' to quickly and efficiently process new information. Schema-based cognition is characterised by the drawing of connections between different pieces of information, allowing individuals to develop holistic understandings of complex systems or concepts.

Xu's (2013) study demonstrates that the cue-based and exemplar-based imagined identities that participating teachers formed during their pre-service training shifted to more rule-based and schema-based practised identities once they began teaching at the novice stage. These changes were influenced by a combination of the institutional contexts of their school environments, which were full of factors influencing social cognition, and the dynamic educational situations they encountered, in which abundant processing of social cognition by teachers occurred. Specifically, the study reports a four-year longitudinal case study of four Chinese EFL teachers during their initial years of teaching. Through this examination, the researcher was able to observe the transformation of the teachers' professional identities over time and document how their social cognition changed as they adapted to their teaching environments and gained experience. The study's findings suggest that the nature of social cognition can undergo significant changes as individuals engage in the active processing of social information related to their professional identity. In this case, the teachers' initial reliance on cue-based and exemplar-based imagined identities gave way to more rule-based and schema-based practised identities as they gained experience and encountered different educational situations. The study's emphasis on the importance of understanding the nature and processes of changes in social cognition over time highlights the need for further research on how individuals' social cognitive processes and identity development occur in various educational and professional contexts. Understanding these changes and the factors influencing them can inform effective professional development programming and teacher education policies which aim to support teachers' identity development and enhance their effectiveness in the classroom.

In summary, this EFL teacher study effectively demonstrates the importance and benefits of researching changes in social cognition for the purpose of understanding its processing.

3.3 Unravelling the Abilities of the Social Mind

Mental representations and cognitive processing are the two major lines of inquiry in social cognition research. However, as these two lines of inquiry intersect in daily life, it has become apparent that a new line of research is necessary: the examination of the abilities of the social mind. Investigating the abilities of the social mind is a synergistic effort that draws on the contributions of both representation-based and processing-based lines of research. In this sense, the ability of the social mind is an individual's ability to understand, process, and use social information effectively in daily life. This ability involves not only cognitive processing but also affective and behavioural components. In this sub-section, we explore how researchers have approached this topic by studying the abilities of the social mind and their role in social interaction.

The abilities of the social mind are critical to our daily social interactions and centre on the individual's ability to monitor and control their own behaviours and cognitions. The self-reflective ability of the social mind is necessary for accurate self-perception and self-awareness; it allows individuals to recognise their own thoughts, feelings, and actions (Farrell, 2022). The cognitive control ability of the social mind permits individuals to regulate their responses to social stimuli and situations, enabling them to flexibly adapt to social contexts. For instance, mindfulness, the ability to stay focused and aware of the present moment without becoming reactive or emotional, is associated with improved cognitive function, emotional regulation, and self-awareness (Yuan et al., 2023). Some abilities, such as self-efficacy, are multifaceted, as they involve both cognitive and affective elements that can be influenced by various factors in one's social life. In this sub-section, we will pay particular attention to reflection, mindfulness, and self-efficacy as three important abilities, amongst many others, of the social mind.

3.3.1 Reflection as the Initiative to Reconstruct

Reflection, as the initiative to reconstruct, is a critical ability of the social mind. It is not just a cognitive process of reviewing past events but an ability that allows individuals to meaningfully engage with their experiences and learn from them. Reflection is a way of reliving in our social mind an experience we have undergone in real social interactions.

For example, consider a school language teacher who reflects on her teaching methods following a lesson. She reconstructs the experience in her mind, considering how she can improve her teaching techniques and better engage students in the lesson. She may consider different approaches to teaching language, reflecting on what worked well and what needed improvement during the lesson. She may identify areas where she needs to improve her teaching methods and make conscious efforts to implement those changes. She can use her reflections to develop new strategies or modify existing ones, making her teaching more effective and engaging for students. In turn, this can help her have a greater impact on the lives of her students, ultimately improving their language skills and overall development.

In language teacher reflection studies, researchers often employ a variety of methods to unravel the complexities of this ability of the social mind. One common method is qualitative research, which involves the use of in-depth interviews and case studies to gain an understanding of language teachers' reflection processes and their impact on teaching practice (Sarab & Mardian, 2023). Qualitative research allows researchers to explore how teachers approach their craft, the challenges they face, and how they reflect on these experiences in order to inform their future actions. Another popular method is cognitive lab-based research, which measures language teachers' cognitive processes during reflection using various experimental techniques. For example, researchers may use think-aloud protocols, eye-tracking technologies, or reaction time measurements to assess how teachers process information, make decisions, and solve problems related to language teaching (e.g., Dagiene et al., 2021). Researchers can also use corpus methods to examine language teachers' reflections on their teaching practice by analysing linguistic patterns in their written reflections or the language they use during interviews (e.g., Urzúa & Asención-Delaney, 2023). For example, researchers can analyse teachers' use of language to identify themes or patterns related to their reflection processes, such as the recurring keywords or particular language structures they use to reflect on their experiences.

Some studies draw on various methods simultaneously, taking a mixed-methods approach to gain a more comprehensive understanding of language teacher reflection. For example, Urzúa and Asención-Delaney (2023) used a mixed-methods approach to explore the reflections of novice Spanish language teachers participating in a weekly blog and video-conferencing session. The study specifically focused on the different types of reflective discourse generated by the teachers – descriptive versus critical – and the themes and categories related to teacher-oriented, learner-oriented, and context-oriented reflections. Blog posts, comments on posts, and videoconference transcripts were all analysed using a mixed-methods approach that combined corpus-based analysis and content discourse analysis. The results show that critical, teacher-oriented reflections predominated in the data but also that there are inherent challenges in expanding the focus of reflections on students' learning. The findings of this study have important implications for language teacher education and professional development, particularly in terms of understanding how teachers' participation in an online community of practice can support their development and the role of critical reflections in that process.

In summary, reflection, as the initiative to reconstruct, is a critical ability of the social mind that empowers us to meaningfully engage and learn from our experiences. It allows us to gain insights into our actions and reactions, extract meaning from our experiences, and use that knowledge to inform our future actions and decisions.

3.3.2 Mindfulness as the Disposition to Concentrate

The ability to concentrate or focus is an essential capability of the social mind, particularly in the context of social interactions. During social interactions, a vast amount of information is constantly pouring into our minds and influencing our cognition, whether this information is in the form of visual cues, auditory signals, or emotional expressions. This information can be either relevant or irrelevant, and it is the ability to concentrate that allows us to filter out the irrelevant information and maintain our focus on the task or goal at hand. Distractions and emotional turbulence can often arise from this deluge of information, making it difficult to maintain a clear and consistent focus. The ability to concentrate, therefore, is in essence the ability to filter out these irrelevant or disruptive influences and keep our attention firmly fixed on the matter at hand. This not only helps us to navigate the complex social landscape but also allows us to respond appropriately and effectively to social cues, maintaining our poise and composure during emotionally charged situations.

For instance, when engaging in a heated debate, the ability to filter out extraneous information such as facial expressions or verbal tics that may trigger emotional reactions can help us to maintain a cool and calculated approach, enabling us to focus on the salient points of the argument and respond in a way that best advances our position. Similarly, when giving a presentation or speech, the ability to concentrate and filter out irrelevant audience noise or movement can help us maintain our train of thought and deliver our message with clarity and precision. For language teachers in particular, the ability to concentrate is crucial in the classroom setting. As language teachers interact with their students, they must constantly filter out irrelevant linguistic input while focusing on students' speech production and language comprehension. This ability helps teachers maintain control of the classroom, identify areas for improvement in their students' language proficiency, and develop targeted teaching strategies that support student learning outcomes. Additionally, language teachers must also filter extraneous emotional cues from their students' facial expressions, tone of voice, and body language that may signal a lack of comprehension or confusion during lessons. This ability not only helps teachers assess students' comprehension but also respond promptly and effectively to students' needs during instruction.

This ability of the social mind to concentrate has been investigated by some researchers who draw on the conceptualisation of teacher mindfulness. For instance, Yuan et al. (2023) conducted a qualitative case study from an ecological perspective to explore how two experienced language teachers' mindfulness (i.e., their ability to concentrate and filter out distracting information) influenced their professional practice and continuous development. The study identified five critical dimensions of teacher mindfulness: self, teaching and learning, professional development, the situated environment, and time and change. It was found that this ability to concentrate constantly interacted with all five dimensions to (re)shape teaching and teacher development. The findings suggest that an explicit focus on this ability should be integrated into teacher education programmes to help teachers cultivate mindful awareness and practice, which can promote both their own well-being and their students' learning.

In summary, the ability to concentrate, for example, by practising mindfulness, is a critical ability of the social mind. It allows us to navigate the complex social world with clarity, purpose, and effectiveness. It is this ability that enables us to filter out irrelevant or disruptive information, allowing us to maintain our focus on the task at hand and to respond appropriately and effectively to the social landscape.

3.3.3 Self-efficacy as the Strength to Persevere

The term self-efficacy refers to individuals' beliefs in their abilities to perform a specific task or behaviour (Bandura, 1997). Therefore, seen through the lens of the ability of the social mind, it can be understood as the strength to persevere in the face of challenges. For instance, when teaching a new language, a teacher with high self-efficacy will approach the task with confidence and determination, believing in their ability to master the material and convey it effectively to students. In language teacher education, it is thus important to consider strategies that enhance teachers' self-efficacy as an ability of their social mind to help them draw upon their inner resources to achieve growth and development.

Social psychologists often rely on cognitive models to gain a better understanding of self-efficacy in their investigations. Cognitive models, which are theoretical frameworks that seek to explain cognitive abilities as reflected or manifested in human cognitive processes, provide social psychologists with a useful tool to explore the complexities of social behaviour. By using cognitive models, social psychologists can identify the cognitive abilities that underlie cognitive processes and how these abilities shape our social interactions. For instance, Wyatt (2016) emphasised the importance of cognitive models for the examination of teachers' self-efficacy (TSE) beliefs and proposed an alternative model based on a reflective learning cycle. The new model was developed on the basis of a qualitative, longitudinal, and multi-case study of English language teachers' practical knowledge and self-efficacy beliefs when participating in an in-service teacher education programme in Oman. The contribution of the study lies not only in the development of the new model but also in the problematisation of the previous model, which had been dominant but appears to be flawed.

The new model links the development of TSE beliefs with practical knowledge (PK) growth and shows how TSE beliefs interact with every stage of a reflective cycle. The model posits that the growth of TSE beliefs is intimately related to PK and that dimensions of PK, such as learners and learning, approaches to teaching, the curriculum, the self, the subject matter, and the broader school context, are drawn upon at each stage of the reflective cycle. The model also emphasises that TSE beliefs need to be understood in relation to other beliefs, orientations, affects, and physiological states that influence the quality and quantity of effort put into any given task. It is important to examine TSE beliefs and other forms of cognition that shape effort in relation to PK to delineate both their degree of fit and their nature (agent-means, means-ends, or agent-ends), as this analysis can influence the selection of teacher education strategies. The model suggests that contexts characterised by 'enriched reflection' can stimulate spiralling growth in PK and TSE beliefs. Reflection and self-doubt are crucial to the processes through which PK and TSE beliefs develop. Relatively fluid task-, domain-, and context-specific TSE beliefs feed into the development of more stable and robust general self-efficacy (GSE) beliefs. Stable GSE beliefs may protect teachers when they are undertaking new tasks for which their TSE beliefs may be low, but perhaps only if the new task is sufficiently similar to previous ones.

In summary, self-efficacy, as the social mind's strength to persevere, is often examined using cognitive models to better understand its components and how they interact to support social cognition. These models can help clarify the beliefs individuals hold about their abilities and how these beliefs impact their behaviour and interactions with others.

4 Social Cognition and Language Teachers

As we discussed in previous sections, the complexities and intricacies of human interaction within a social environment are explored in research in the realm of social cognition, with an emphasis on how individuals process information and use it to guide their behaviour. This section delves deeper into the specific case of language teachers, examining how their social cognition impacts their teaching practices and thus the learning experiences of their students. It highlights how language teachers' social cognition shapes their understanding of social situations within the classroom and their responses to these situations. Drawing from a range of research studies, this section illustrates how language teachers' social cognition is not only integral to their professional development but also crucial for fostering a learning environment that is conducive to language acquisition and cultural understanding. Specifically, this section is divided into two sub-sections. The first sub-section focuses on language teachers' social cognition of teaching, exploring how they perceive, interpret, and make sense of social interactions in the classroom. The second sub-section examines their social cognition in relation to teachers' learning and development, investigating how they understand and navigate the social dynamics of professional growth and learning communities. By delving into these two aspects of social cognition, we aim to gain a comprehensive understanding of how language teachers' social cognition shapes their teaching practices and professional development.

4.1 Language Teachers' Social Cognition and Teaching

This sub-section introduces two different yet related perspectives on language teachers' social cognition of teaching. We first focus on understanding how teachers' beliefs, attitudes, and social and educational environments influence their views on teaching. This highlights the complex interplay between individual cognition and the societal factors that shape language teaching practices. In contrast, the second sub-section shifts the focus to the cognitive processes underlying language teachers' social cognition, exploring how teachers process information in practice and how they make decisions based on what they know, think, and believe. Both sub-sections highlight the importance of examining teachers' views of teaching, as part of their social cognition, from multiple perspectives to gain a comprehensive understanding of the complexities involved in language teaching practices.

4.1.1 Language Teachers' Views of Teaching

Numerous studies have delved into language teachers' social cognition and teachers' views of language teaching in particular, although not all these studies explicitly profess to adopt a social cognitive viewpoint. These studies often centre on themes such as teachers' beliefs, attitudes, and interactions within their social and educational environments, aiming to unpack the complex interplay between individual cognition and the societal factors that shape language teaching practices.

For instance, Sun et al. (2022) introduce a new way to understand how Chinese teachers of English feel about a more communication-based approach to teaching, compared to more traditional methods. They call this innovative new method the Implicit Association Test (IAT). The IAT helps researchers tap into teachers' unconscious biases and preferences to understand what they really think and believe, even if they do not say it outright. It is based on the idea that teachers make decisions based on what they know, think, and believe. The researchers used the IAT to study twenty-four Chinese teachers of English who had all attended the same teacher training school and now taught at different levels in the same city. The results reveal a spectrum of implicit preferences for communication-oriented teaching, showing that these teachers had different levels of preference for the communication-based approach over the traditional one. Interestingly, the study found that what some teachers said in interviews did not always match what the IAT revealed they really thought. A noteworthy finding was the disconnect between some teachers' stated beliefs in interviews and their actual implicit attitudes, as uncovered by the IAT. This disconnect, the researchers posit, could stem from a complex interplay of personal, institutional, and societal factors that subtly influence teaching practices. By shedding light on these hidden cognitions, the study not only adds a new dimension to understanding teacher decision-making but also underscores the importance of such insights in tailoring effective curriculum reforms.

Rahimi and Ong's (2023) study strives to offer a deeper understanding of how learning English as a foreign language can be made more captivating and productive. The researchers accomplished this by delving into the teaching approaches and methods of five accomplished teachers, as well as the learning experiences of their seventy-nine students. Data was gathered through interviews, classroom observations, and group discussions. Data analysis revealed that these teachers possessed a profound and well-connected knowledge of teaching speaking skills and could effectively put this knowledge into practice. The students, in turn, saw their teachers as approachable and skilled mentors. Importantly, the teachers' techniques and actions allowed their students to form close-knit study groups, take ownership of their learning, and enjoy completing various meaningful tasks. Overall, the students felt that their learning experiences met their psychological needs for independence, ability, and a sense of belonging, leading to increased participation in language learning on multiple levels – behavioural, cognitive, emotional, and social. These results build upon previous studies and have valuable implications for the field of language education.

This study is closely related to teachers' social cognition in several ways. In the context of teaching, teachers' social cognition involves their understanding of social dynamics in the classroom, their perceptions of students' needs and abilities, and their ability to adapt their teaching practices accordingly. In this study, the researchers explored the cognition and practices of expert teachers, focusing on how they created engaging and effective learning opportunities for their students. This necessarily involved understanding the social aspects of teaching, such as how teachers perceive their students' needs, how they establish relationships with them, and how they design classroom activities that foster positive social interactions. By examining teachers' practices through interviews, observations, and focus groups, the researchers gained insights into their social cognitive processes. For example, they found that expert teachers possessed detailed knowledge of teaching speaking skills and could effectively translate this knowledge into practice. This suggests that they had a sophisticated understanding of the social demands of language learning and were able to scaffold students' learning in ways that are socially and emotionally supportive. Furthermore, the study found that teachers' behaviours and practices created opportunities for students to form cohesive groups, exercise their agency, and enjoy completing meaningful activities. This indicates that teachers' social cognition plays a crucial role in creating a positive classroom environment that fosters student engagement and learning. Although it is not explicitly stated, this study is related to teachers' social cognition because it examines how teachers' understanding of social dynamics in the classroom influences their teaching practices and, ultimately, students' learning experiences. By shedding light on these processes, the study contributes to our understanding of effective teaching practices and the role of social cognition in language education.

Several similarities and differences emerge when comparing this study with that of Sun et al. (2022), particularly with regard to their respective scopes, methodologies, and focal points. One significant similarity is that both studies share a common goal: to understand how teachers' perspectives, underpinned by their social cognition, shape classroom practices and, ultimately, student learning outcomes. Both studies recognise that teachers' beliefs and attitudes, as elements of their social cognition, are crucial factors in determining their teaching styles and approaches, which in turn impact students' learning outcomes. However, a notable difference lies in the scope and focus of each study. While Sun et al. (2022) compared teachers' attitudes towards two different teaching methods (communication-based vs. traditional), Rahimi and Ong (2023) take a broader view, exploring not just teaching methods but also the overall learning environment created by expert teachers and its impact on students' engagement and psychological needs. Furthermore, Rahimi and Ong (2023) delve into students' perspectives, examining their experiences, perceptions of their teachers, and levels of engagement. This aspect is particularly significant as it highlights the importance of student-centred approaches in language education. By contrast, Sun et al. (2022) primarily focus on teachers' cognition, with students' perspectives playing a secondary role. Both studies contribute to the field of language education by providing insights into effective teaching practices and learning environments. However, Rahimi and Ong (2023) extend previous research by offering a more holistic view that encompasses not just teaching methods but also the social and emotional dimensions of language learning. Additionally, while Sun et al. (2022) employ the Implicit Association Test (IAT) to capture teachers' implicit attitudes and beliefs towards communication-based teaching, Rahimi and Ong (2023) rely on a more qualitative approach, utilising semi-structured interviews, observations, and focus-group discussions to explore expert teachers' cognitions and practices as well as students' experiences and engagement.

Such studies have several implications for future research on teachers' views of language teaching from a social cognitive perspective. Firstly, they highlight the importance of understanding teachers' beliefs, attitudes, and interactions within their social and educational environments. This suggests that future research should focus on exploring how teachers' social cognitive processes influence their teaching practices. For example, researchers may investigate how teachers' social identities, cultural backgrounds, and professional communities shape their views on language teaching. Secondly, studies like that produced by Sun et al. (2022) demonstrate the potential of innovative methods like the Implicit Association Test (IAT) as a way of revealing teachers' implicit beliefs and attitudes. This suggests that future research could explore the use of similar methods to gain a more comprehensive understanding of teachers' social cognition. For instance, researchers could investigate how teachers' implicit biases about language learning or teaching may influence their practices. Finally, these studies emphasise the need to consider the complex interplay between individual cognition and the societal factors that shape language teaching practices. This suggests that future research should aim to unpack the mechanisms underlying this interplay, such as how teachers' personal beliefs interact with broader social and cultural forces to shape their teaching practices.

In conclusion, these studies offer implications for future research on teachers' views of language teaching from a social cognitive perspective by emphasising the importance of understanding teachers' social cognitive processes, exploring innovative methods to reveal their implicit beliefs and attitudes, and considering the complex interplay between individual cognition and the societal factors that shape teaching practices.

4.1.2 Language Teachers' Thinking about Teaching

In the previous sub-section, we discussed studies examining teachers' views of language teaching within the framework of social cognition. These investigations centre on understanding teachers' beliefs, attitudes, and how their social and educational environments influence their perspectives. In this sub-section, we shift our focus to explore studies on teachers' thinking about language teaching. Specifically, we delve into the cognitive processes that underlie language teachers' social cognition – how they process information, make decisions, and solve problems related to language instruction. By exploring teachers' thought processes, we aim to gain a deeper understanding of the complex mental activities that shape their teaching practices and, ultimately, student learning outcomes.

For instance, Fagan (2015) looked at how an experienced English as a Second Language (ESL) teacher thought about her classroom practices when responding to students' questions in real time. The researcher wanted to know how this kind of thinking might change the teacher's understanding of teaching language, even after many years of teaching. To elucidate this, the researcher combined two research methods: conversation analysis and ethnographic analysis. The findings indicate that the teacher used two different approaches when answering students' questions: answering them directly and showing the students how to find the answer themselves. The researcher looked closely at how these approaches worked and what kinds of verbal and non-verbal cues influenced their use. The findings show that many different factors affected how the teacher handled students' questions. Some of these factors were in line with her ideas about teaching, while others were not. The study ends with a discussion about how the findings connect to what we already know about teacher cognition, and how they suggest that we need to use more diverse research methods to better understand how teachers learn.

Fagan's (2015) study is deeply connected to the concept of teachers' social cognition, particularly in relation to their thought processes – which are revealed to be a crucial aspect of their social cognition. When addressing learner inquiries, for instance, the teacher must quickly analyse the situation, interpret the student's needs, and formulate a response that is both educationally effective and sensitive to the social context. This process requires a complex set of cognitive skills that includes problem-solving, decision-making, and metacognition (i.e., thinking about one's own thinking). By examining an expert ESL teacher's micro-analysis of her classroom practices, this study sheds light on the inner workings of teachers' social cognition. It demonstrates how teachers' thought processes are shaped by their engagement with social activities and how these processes, in turn, influence their teaching practices. The findings of this study not only contribute to our understanding of teacher cognition but also highlight the importance of considering teachers' thought processes when designing educational interventions and professional development programmes.

Yin's (2010) study examines the inner thought processes of teachers during assessments. Specifically, this study explores the cognitive processes of two English for Academic Purposes (EAP) instructors at a university language centre in the UK. The researcher gathered data through various methods, including observing teachers in the classroom, conducting interviews, and using stimulated recall techniques. The findings of the study reveal the diverse cognitive strategies that teachers employ when assessing their students' language skills. These strategies range from analysing students' performance to drawing upon the teacher's own experiences and knowledge. Based on these insights, the paper offers practical suggestions for enhancing the effectiveness of classroom assessment practices. The study also highlights the significant influence of managerialism on teachers' assessment-related decisions. It also delves into the social construction of student language ability within the classroom context, emphasising the importance of considering students' social and cultural backgrounds when assessing their language proficiency. Overall, this paper provides valuable insights into the complex cognitive processes involved in classroom language assessment and has practical implications for the improvement of teaching and learning outcomes.

Evidently, this study is also deeply related to teachers' social cognition, particularly in terms of their thought processes during classroom language assessment. The study explores the cognitive processes of teachers during classroom assessments, which necessarily involves social cognition. When teachers assess students' language skills, they draw upon their own knowledge and experiences, as well as their understanding of students' backgrounds, abilities, and efforts. This requires teachers to engage in complex cognitive tasks such as analysing student performance, comparing it to standards or expectations, and making judgments about students' progress. Importantly, the study highlights how teachers' thinking processes are influenced by managerialism and the social construction of students' language ability within the classroom. This suggests that teachers' social cognition is shaped not only by their personal beliefs and experiences but also by the broader educational and societal contexts in which they operate. Therefore, this study provides valuable insights into the role of social cognition in teachers' thinking processes during classroom assessments. It underscores the importance of considering teachers' cognitive strategies and the social and cultural factors that influence their assessment-related decisions. By doing so, we can better understand how teachers make sense of and respond to students' performance in the classroom, which has important implications for the improvement of teaching and learning outcomes.

By and large, both Fagan's (2015) study and Yin's (2010) study are similar in that they explore the relation between teachers' thought processes and their social cognition. Both seek to understand how teachers process and interpret information in social situations, particularly within the classroom context. More specifically, the main similarity between the two papers is their focus on teachers' cognition and how it shapes their interactions with students and teaching practices. Both studies recognise that understanding teachers' thought processes is crucial for understanding their behaviour in the classroom and improving their effectiveness as teachers. However, there are also notable differences between the two studies. Fagan's (2015) study examines an expert ESL teacher's micro-analysis of her classroom practices when addressing learner inquiries, with a focus on how such analysis led to changes in her conscious awareness of teaching language. It uses conversation analysis and ethnographic analysis to detail the teacher's practices and the factors that influenced them. On the other hand, Yin's (2010) study explores teachers' thought processes in the specific context of conducting classroom language assessment. It employs case studies of two EAP instructors, and data was collected through classroom observations, interviews, and stimulated recall. This study identifies various forms of cognition that teachers use when assessing students and considers how managerialism and the social construction of student language ability influence these processes. In summary, while both studies investigate teachers' thought processes as elements of their social cognition, they differ in their focus: the first study looks at how teachers respond to learner inquiries, and the second study examines teachers' assessment practices and the underlying cognitive processes that inform these practices.

The two studies showcased above are excellent examples of studies inquiring into language teachers' social cognitive processes and offer valuable insights for future research. Firstly, they highlight the importance of understanding teachers' beliefs, attitudes, and how their social and educational environments shape their perspectives. This understanding can help identify potential barriers to effective teaching and learning and contribute to the development of strategies to address them. Secondly, the studies shed light on the cognitive strategies teachers employ when conducting classroom teaching, for example, during classroom assessments. Future research could delve deeper into these strategies, examining how they vary among teachers and how they can be enhanced through professional development. Additionally, researchers could investigate how teachers' cognitive processes evolve over time as they gain experience, thus providing insights into teacher development trajectories. Future research could also build upon these existing studies by exploring a wider range of aspects of teachers' social cognitive processes. For instance, researchers could delve deeper into how teachers' beliefs about language learning inform their selection of specific instructional techniques. By examining the relationship between teachers' beliefs and their actual teaching practices, researchers may gain insights into the cognitive processes that guide teachers' decision-making. These cognitive processes reflect the mental activities involved in perceiving, interpreting, and responding to various teaching situations. For instance, a teacher who believes in the importance of student-centred learning might design activities that encourage active participation and collaboration, reflecting a cognitive process that prioritises learner engagement. In essence, understanding the link between teachers' beliefs and their teaching practices can open a window into their cognitive processes, which is crucial for finding ways to encourage effective language instruction. This understanding can help researchers and educators identify areas where a teacher's thinking aligns with best practices in language education and areas where additional support or professional development may be needed to enhance their effectiveness as a teacher. Moreover, studies could also investigate the intersections between teachers' social cognition and other critical aspects of their professional identity, such as their sense of self as educators or their approach to lifelong learning. By examining these intersections, we may gain a more comprehensive understanding of the complex interplay between teachers' cognitive processes, professional identities, and teaching practices. Such insights can inform efforts to help teachers develop more effective and authentic teaching styles that align with their beliefs and values. In conclusion, by continuing to refine our understanding of teachers' social cognitive processes, we can better support them in their professional development and ultimately improve student learning outcomes in language teaching.

4.2 Language Teacher's Social Cognition and Teacher Development

In their pursuit of professional excellence, language teachers undergo a continuous process of development that encompasses both their knowledge and emotional growth. In this sub-section, we explore this dynamic aspect of teachers' professional journeys, highlighting how their intellectual and emotional capacities are intricately linked to their social cognition. By examining the intersection of knowledge, competence, and emotional intelligence in teaching, this sub-section reveals the critical role of social cognition in promoting language teachers' development.

4.2.1 Developing Knowledge and Competence

As language teachers continue to develop their knowledge and competence, their social cognition plays an increasingly active role. In other words, the development of knowledge and competence among language teachers is closely intertwined with their social cognition. As language teachers gain more experience and expertise, they develop a deeper understanding of the complexities involved in teaching a language. This understanding includes not only linguistic knowledge but also insights into cultural differences, learning styles, and student motivation. Teachers' social cognition thus influences how they interpret these complexities and guides their instructional decisions. For example, a teacher with strong social cognition might be more likely to notice when a student is struggling with a particular concept due to cultural differences or learning style preferences. This teacher would then be able to modify their teaching approach to better meet the students' needs. In this way, the development of knowledge and competence among language teachers feeds into their social cognition and is also shaped by it. As teachers continue to grow and learn, their social cognition becomes more refined and nuanced, enabling them to teach more effectively in diverse and challenging educational environments.

For instance, Li and Xu (2021) aimed to understand what kinds of knowledge EFL teachers use when selecting and utilising teaching materials. The researchers drew from theories about how people use tools and how foreign language teachers combine teaching methods with subject knowledge. They conducted a detailed study involving eight EFL teachers at a Chinese university. Over three semesters, they collected data through interviews, classroom observations, and document analysis. Their findings show that teachers' knowledge about the use of materials is complex and evolves as they gain more experience. This knowledge can be grouped into four main areas: subject matter (i.e., what is being taught), teaching methods, curriculum planning, and the classroom context. Importantly, the researchers found that this professional knowledge is not just personal; it is influenced by interactions with other people and the materials themselves. Both teachers and materials play a role in its development. Based on their findings, the researchers provide suggestions for how teachers might learn more effectively by using materials in their language classrooms.

Li and Xu's (2021) study thus examines the complex relationship between EFL teachers' knowledge and their use of teaching materials. Their analysis provides a fascinating window into the reciprocal relationship between teachers' learning and their social cognition, as teachers draw upon and develop their professional knowledge in the process of selecting and utilising educational resources. Firstly, the study recognises that teachers' knowledge about the use of materials is multi-dimensional and developmental. This aligns with the idea that cognition – in this case, teachers' understanding of how to effectively use materials – constantly evolves as teachers engage with new challenges and experiences in the classroom. The four domains of knowledge identified in the study (subject matter, pedagogical, curricular, and contextual) reflect the breadth of understanding required for the effective use of materials, indicating that teachers must continually adapt and refine their approaches based on the specific demands of each lesson or context. Secondly, the study's finding that professional knowledge about the use of materials is mediated by both human and non-human elements underscores the interactive nature of teaching and learning. Teachers do not operate in isolation; rather, they constantly negotiate meaning and purpose with their students, their colleagues, and the materials themselves. This process of negotiation requires teachers to be highly attuned to the needs and capabilities of their learners, as well as the affordances and limitations of the materials at hand. In this way, teaching becomes a dynamic exchange between teachers' social cognition and the various elements that constitute the learning environment. Finally, the researchers' emphasis on new forms of agency speaks to the reciprocal relationship between teachers' learning and their social cognition. As teachers expand their understanding of how materials can be used effectively, they necessarily transform their teaching practices to accommodate new insights and strategies. Conversely, the materials themselves – through their design, content, and affordances – can influence how teachers approach their craft and what they come to understand as effective practice. In this sense, teachers' learning and their social cognition are mutually constitutive; each shapes and is shaped by the other in an ongoing cycle of growth and development. In conclusion, this study provides compelling evidence for the reciprocal relationship between teachers' learning and their social cognition as manifested in EFL teachers' use of materials. By examining how teachers draw upon and develop their professional knowledge in the context of material use, we gain a deeper understanding of the complex interplay between cognitive processes and instructional practices that characterises effective language teaching and teacher learning.

Poh's (2021) study also showcases how teachers' learning, and their development of knowledge and competence in particular, is reciprocally related to their social cognition. Guided by a sociocultural approach to teacher learning that underscores the social basis of human cognition, the study presents a qualitative examination of how sociocultural factors shape the teaching practices of three beginner teachers in Singapore's secondary schools. The results highlight the need to account for broader social structures when analysing teachers' classroom behaviours and interactions. The study concludes by discussing the implications of its results for the improvement of teacher education programmes.

This study clearly reflects the reciprocal relationship between teachers' learning and their social cognition by examining how the social and cultural context in which teachers operate influences their teaching practices. The focus is on novice teachers in Singaporean secondary schools, and the aim is to understand the sociocultural influences on their teaching. The sociocultural perspective on teacher learning, a perspective that involves not only teachers' social cognition but also their social interactions in specific contexts, emphasises the social origin of human cognition, recognising that individuals' knowledge and skills are developed and shaped within their social and cultural contexts. The findings demonstrate that larger structures, such as educational policies, school cultures, and community expectations, play a significant role in shaping teachers' speech and actions in the classroom. These structures influence how teachers interpret and implement teaching practices, as well as their beliefs about effective teaching. By taking into account the role of these larger structures, the study highlights the need to consider the social and cultural context in which teachers operate when analysing their classroom practices. This, in turn, has implications for teacher education, suggesting that teacher preparation programmes should go beyond merely advocating particular teaching practices and instead help teachers develop the ability to navigate and adapt to the social and cultural demands of their teaching contexts. In summary, this study reflects the reciprocal relationship between teacher learning and social cognition by emphasising the influence of social and cultural factors on teachers' cognitive processes and teaching practices.

The two studies described above share some commonalities, but also have important differences. Both studies focus on teacher learning and its relationship with social cognition, emphasising the role of social and cultural factors in shaping teachers' practices and beliefs; both adopt a qualitative approach, utilising interviews, observations, and other qualitative methods to collect data and understand teachers' experiences and perspectives; and both recognise the importance of context in understanding teachers' practices. They acknowledge that teaching does not occur in isolation but is influenced by the broader social, cultural, and institutional environments. However, they also have important differences. While Li and Xu (2021) appear to focus on a specific aspect of teachers' learning or social cognition, Poh (2021) seems to extend this focus to investigate the reciprocal relationship between teachers' learning and social cognition more broadly. Poh (2021) considers how teachers' learning is shaped by their social interactions and cultural contexts and how, in turn, their learning influences their social cognition and behaviour in the classroom. Poh's (2021) study also differs in its specific focus on novice teachers in Singaporean secondary schools, whereas Li and Xu's (2021) study examined teachers at different career stages or in different educational settings. Poh's (2021) focus allows for a more nuanced understanding of the specific challenges and opportunities facing novice teachers in this particular context. Finally, the findings and implications of the two studies differ due to differences in their specific research questions and methodologies. While both studies aim to understand the influence of social and cultural factors on teachers' practice, they arrive at different conclusions or recommendations based on their unique findings and analytical frameworks. In summary, while the two studies share some common ground in terms of their focus on teachers' learning and social cognition, they differ in their broader scopes, specific contexts, findings, and implications.

Future research should aim to explore two particular areas in depth. Firstly, there is a need to investigate which specific types of knowledge and competence are most susceptible to shifts in teachers' social cognition as they engage with the multifaceted challenges of classroom teaching. This will help us understand how the evolution of teachers' social understanding impacts their professional capabilities. Secondly, additional research efforts should be directed towards elucidating and analysing the precise social cognitive processes employed by language teachers to facilitate distinct stages of teacher learning. Currently, the available literature lacks a nuanced examination of the interconnected processes involved in this phenomenon. Further endeavours are anticipated to describe and analyse the specific social cognitive processes that are conducive to certain specific processes of teacher learning. In other words, the existing literature does not seem to provide a detailed account of process-to-process dynamics.

Such an exploration could significantly enhance our comprehension of how teachers learn and adapt within their social and educational environments.

4.2.2 Promoting Emotional Growth

In the preceding sub-section, we delved into the reciprocal relationship between language teachers' development of knowledge and competence and their evolving social cognition. This intricate interplay is not only intellectual in nature but also deeply emotional, as teachers navigate the complexities of the classroom while fostering a learning environment. In this sub-section, we shift our focus to explore the connection between teachers' emotional growth and their social cognition. Emotions play a pivotal role in teaching, shaping how teachers perceive and respond to the social dynamics of the classroom (Day & Gu, 2009). As such, understanding the emotional landscape of teaching and how it intersects with social cognition is crucial for supporting teachers in their professional journey. By exploring this relationship, we aim to shed light on the emotional labour involved in teaching and its impact on teachers' personal and professional growth.

A relevant study by Kiel et al. (2016) aims to pinpoint future special education teachers (SETs) who might struggle with job-related stresses and demands. It is not difficult to imagine that SETs face more stress than teachers in regular schools. In fact, SETs are often more likely to leave the profession than other teachers. That is why this study zeroes in on 'dysfunctional cognition' – thoughts that can heighten stress in tough work situations and harm health over time. By understanding these unhelpful thought patterns, we can develop ways to support student teachers who have a low tolerance for stress. This study looks at 333 student teachers in the German educational system working with students who have special needs, such as learning difficulties, mental health issues, emotional or social challenges, or sensory disabilities (e.g., hearing loss or speech problems). Using statistical methods such as hierarchical cluster analysis and discriminant analysis, the researchers delineated four distinct groups of student teachers based on their dysfunctional cognition. The first group had the fewest unhelpful thoughts. The second and third groups exhibited higher levels of such thoughts, especially those involving feelings of dependency, internalising failure, and setting impossibly high standards (or perfectionism). The fourth group had the highest levels of dysfunctional cognition. Interestingly, having fewer unhelpful thoughts (except for perfectionism) tended to go hand-in-hand with a stronger sense of self-efficacy. Moreover, no single group defined all student teachers working in a specific special needs area. For instance, student teachers working with mentally disabled students tended to fall into the third group, with their high levels of thoughts involving internalised failure and dependency. Those working with students affected by emotional or social disorders often fell into the fourth group – the 'risk' group. These findings can inform the design of effective support strategies for student teachers who might struggle in stressful work environments and may need extra training and careful career guidance to help them succeed.

This study is clearly highly relevant to the reciprocal relationship between teachers' emotions and their social cognition. Firstly, it recognises the significant and stressful burdens faced by SETs, which are often exacerbated by forms of dysfunctional cognition that can amplify stress responses in challenging occupational settings. These dysfunctional cognitive processes, in turn, can have long-term detrimental effects on teachers' health and well-being. Importantly, this study identifies specific clusters of different forms of dysfunctional cognition among prospective SETs, highlighting how these cognitive patterns vary across different areas of special needs education. This variation suggests that SETs' social cognition – how they perceive and interpret social situations and interactions in the classroom – may be shaped by the unique demands and challenges of their particular educational context. Furthermore, the findings emphasise the importance of addressing teachers' emotional growth and resilience. By identifying those student teachers who may struggle with occupational stress, the study paves the way for the development of targeted support measures such as additional training or balanced career counselling. These interventions can help teachers cultivate more adaptive forms of social cognition and emotional coping strategies, enabling them to navigate the complexities of the classroom more effectively. In summary, this study underscores the intricate relationship between teachers' emotions, social cognition, and occupational stress in the context of special needs education. By shedding light on this relationship, the study highlights the need for comprehensive support systems that foster emotional growth and resilience among teachers, ultimately enhancing their ability to provide high-quality education to students with special needs.

Hiver's (2017) study is another excellent example of research on the interplay between teachers' emotional growth and their social cognition. This study uses Retrodictive Qualitative Modelling, a research method that analyses phenomena from a changing and real-life point of view. The goal is to build solid evidence for a new idea called 'language teacher immunity'. To do this, the study brought together 44 focus groups made up of second language (L2) teachers and teacher trainers. It also examined survey data from 293 K-12 language teachers to find common patterns or 'archetypes' related to teacher immunity. Eighteen teachers who fitted these archetypes were then interviewed in depth to understand how their thoughts and teaching practices changed over time and how this immunity showed up in their work. The results suggest that teacher immunity is linked to how teachers feel, think, and act in the social setting of the L2 classroom. This study helps us understand how language teachers can stay flexible, open to change, mentally healthy, and committed to their students' learning. The concept of teacher immunity helps to connect different ideas about the training of L2 teachers and the psychology of language teaching and learning.

This study is clearly related to the reciprocal relationship between teachers' emotional growth and their social cognition. In essence, emotions and social cognition are intricately linked. Our emotions influence how we perceive and interpret social cues, and in turn, our social cognition shapes our emotional responses. This interplay is particularly relevant in the context of teaching, where teachers' emotions and social cognition jointly impact their interactions with students and the learning environment. In Hiver's (2017) study, the concept of 'language teacher immunity' serves as a lens through which to examine this relationship. Teacher immunity, as previously mentioned, encompasses teachers' psychological, emotional, and cognitive functioning in the L2 classroom. By investigating how teachers navigate challenges, maintain their well-being, and remain invested in their students' learning, the study indirectly sheds light on their emotional growth. Crucially, this emotional growth is closely tied to teachers' social cognition. As teachers develop a deeper understanding of their own emotions and those of their students, they become better equipped to perceive and interpret social cues accurately. This enhanced social cognition allows them to build stronger relationships with students, create more inclusive learning environments, and respond more effectively to their students' needs. The methodology employed in this study, which included focus groups, questionnaires, and in-depth interviews, provides rich data that illuminate this relationship. For instance, through in-depth interviews with representative teachers from different archetypes, the study traces developmental trajectories and explores how teachers manifest their emotional growth as motivated thoughts and instructional practices. This analysis reveals how teachers' emotions shape their social cognition and vice versa. In summary, the study contributes to a deeper understanding of the reciprocal relationship between teachers' emotional growth and their social cognition by examining the concept of language teacher immunity and its empirical manifestations. Through this lens, we can appreciate how emotions and social cognition jointly influence teachers' effectiveness in the classroom and their ability to foster positive learning outcomes for students.

The two studies discussed above share some commonalities and some differences. Both studies focus on teachers, specifically those working in challenging environments, and both employ qualitative and quantitative methodologies. Kiel et al. (2016) used hierarchical cluster analysis and discriminant analysis, while Hiver (2017) used focus groups, questionnaire data, cluster analysis, and serial in-depth interviews. Both studies aimed to identify specific groups or archetypes among the participating teachers, and both recognise the importance of teachers' psychological well-being and its impact on their ability to cope with occupational stress. Kiel et al. (2016) focuses on dysfunctional cognitions as a source of stress, while Hiver (2017) emphasises teacher immunity as a factor contributing to psychological well-being and adaptivity. There are also notable differences between the two studies. Firstly, their theoretical frameworks differ. Kiel et al. (2016) focuses on dysfunctional cognitions as a basis for developing supportive measures, while Hiver (2017) uses Retrodictive Qualitative Modelling to establish an empirical foundation for the new construct of language teacher immunity. Secondly, the specific outcomes of the studies differ. Kiel et al. (2016) aimed to identify SETs who might have difficulties coping with occupational stresses, while Hiver (2017) aimed to validate the construct of language teacher immunity and its association with teachers' psychological, emotional, and cognitive functioning. Additionally, the studies differ slightly in scope. While both focus on teachers' ability to cope with occupational demands, Kiel et al. (2016) are more narrowly focused on dysfunctional cognitions and their impact on stress levels. Hiver (2017) takes a broader approach, examining teacher immunity as a multifaceted construct that encompasses psychological, emotional, and cognitive functioning in the social setting of the L2 classroom.

Looking ahead, two promising directions for future research on the interplay between teachers' emotional growth and their social cognition emerge. Firstly, given the breadth of the emotional domain, there is a pressing need to delve deeper into the specific emotional factors that might explicitly or implicitly shape teachers' social cognitive processes. This may involve exploring how different emotions, such as joy, frustration, or empathy, can influence a teacher's ability to perceive and interpret social cues, as well as how these emotions might mediate changes in teachers' social cognition over time. By unpacking the nuances of emotional experiences within the teaching profession, researchers can gain a more refined understanding of how emotions inform and are informed by social cognitive processes. Secondly, it is crucial to examine the features of this interplay that are unique to language teachers. Language teaching is inherently both social and emotionally charged, and thus requires teachers to navigate complex interpersonal dynamics and cultural sensitivities. Future studies could explore how the specific demands and challenges of language teaching shape the relationship between emotional growth and social cognition, potentially revealing insights that are distinct from those found in other educational settings. By honing in on the specificities of language teachers' experiences, research could contribute to the development of more tailored support strategies and professional development opportunities that foster both emotional well-being and social cognitive proficiency in this vital professional group.

5 Social Cognition and Language Teacher Development

In the preceding sections of this Element, we delved into the intricate realm of language teachers' social cognition. Sections 2 and 3 provided a conceptual framework and methodological approaches for examining language teachers' social cognition, laying the foundation for an understanding of how teachers' social cognition shapes their interactions with students and informs their teaching practices. Section 4, building upon this foundation, illuminated the research landscape by showcasing exemplary studies that investigate language teachers' social cognition in action.

Now, as we turn to Section 5, our attention shifts to the future of this emerging field. In this section, we explore what remains to be discovered about language teachers' social cognition. We will consider how future research might push the boundaries of our current understanding, inquiring deeper into the complexities of teachers' social cognitive processes and their impact on teaching and learning. Moreover, we will also discuss the implications of our growing knowledge for teacher education practice, highlighting how insights from social cognition research can inform the design of more effective teacher preparation and professional development programmes.

5.1 Knowledge and Competence

In the field of language education, the terms 'knowledge' and 'competence' are sometimes used interchangeably, but they carry distinct meanings. Knowledge, in this context, refers to the conceptual understanding that teachers possess with regard to the teaching and learning of languages (Edge & Garton, 2009). It encompasses, for instance, subject matter expertise, pedagogical content knowledge, and an understanding of how language is acquired and used in different contexts. Competence, on the other hand, is the ability to apply this knowledge effectively in teaching situations, demonstrating proficiency in classroom management, assessment, and the facilitation of student learning (Sercu et al., 2005). It is important to note that while knowledge is essential, it is the application of this knowledge – the translation of theory into practice – that constitutes true competence.

As we inquire into the topic of 'knowledge and competence' in relation to language teachers' social cognition, a key approach to future research and teacher education practice emerges. This approach centres on finding an interface between general research on teacher cognition and more specific research on teachers' social cognition. Analysis of this intersection promises a deeper understanding of how teachers' social interactions and relationships with students shape their teaching practices. By bridging these two areas of research, we can gain insights into how teachers' cognitive processes – including their beliefs, decision-making, and reflective practices – are influenced by their social environments.

5.1.1 Suggestions for Future Research

Previous research on language teacher cognition, while providing valuable insights into teachers' thought processes and decision-making, has often suffered from a lack of specificity and a tendency to overlook the social dimensions of teaching. These studies have tended to paint a broad picture of the factors that influence teachers' cognition, such as their beliefs, knowledge, and experiences, without fully acknowledging the social nature of these factors. As a result, they may have failed to capture the complex social interactions and relationships that are integral to the teaching and learning processes. To illustrate this point, while previous research has examined how teachers' beliefs about language learning influence their classroom practices (e.g., Zheng, 2015), it has often neglected to consider how these beliefs are shaped and negotiated within the social context of the classroom. Similarly, studies have looked at how teachers' knowledge impacts their ability to plan and implement effective lessons (e.g., Xu, 2015), but have not always explored how this knowledge is constructed and shared through social interactions with students and other teachers. This oversight is problematic because it results in an underestimation of the significance of the social cognitive dimension in language teaching and learning. It is through social interactions that teachers negotiate meaning, collaborate, and learn from their peers and students. Therefore, a more comprehensive understanding of language teachers' cognition should incorporate a social cognitive perspective to fully capture the complexity and richness of teaching and learning in social contexts.

Incorporating the social cognitive perspective into teacher cognition research can lead to more nuanced and context-specific understandings. For instance, when examining language teachers' attitudes towards multilingualism researchers can explore how teachers' understandings of the social nature of language influence their classroom practices. Teachers who operate in multilingual societies often view language not just as a school subject, but also as a tool for communication and expression. They recognise that students draw from their entire linguistic repertoire to articulate ideas and make sense of the world around them. These teachers are more likely to encourage translanguaging – the use of multiple languages for classroom interactions – because they understand that it fosters inclusivity, creativity, and critical thinking (Li, 2024). They see language learning as inseparable from students' lived experiences and intellectual development (Creese & Blackledge, 2015). On the other hand, teachers who primarily view the language they teach as a discrete school subject – akin to mathematics, science, or social studies – may be less likely to integrate multiple languages into their instruction. They may perceive translanguaging as a distraction or a barrier to learning the target language, rather than recognising its potential to enhance comprehension and engagement (Shan & Xu, 2023). By exploring these differing perspectives, researchers can gain a deeper understanding of the social dimensions of teacher cognition. They can investigate how teachers' beliefs and attitudes about multilingualism are shaped by their social contexts and how these beliefs, in turn, influence their teaching practices. Such an approach may provide a more comprehensive and context-sensitive analysis of teacher cognition, illuminating the complex dynamics that underlie teachers' thoughts, decisions, and actions in the classroom.

To summarise these research gaps, previous research on language teacher cognition has offered valuable insights but often lacks specificity and neglects the social dimensions of teaching. This oversight is problematic because it results in an underestimation of the significance of social interactions in shaping teachers' beliefs, knowledge, and practices. To address this gap, future research should adopt a social cognitive perspective that allows it to explore how teachers' cognition is influenced by and negotiated within the social context of the classroom. For instance, studies could investigate how teachers' understandings of the social nature of language impact their attitudes towards multilingualism and classroom practices. By exploring the social dimension of teacher cognition, researchers may gain a more detailed and context-specific understanding of teaching and learning processes. Such an approach could illuminate the complex dynamics that underlie teachers' thoughts, decisions, and actions, leading to more effective and inclusive language education practices.

5.1.2 Suggestions for Teacher Education Practice

Teacher education practice should incorporate the social dimension into the design of both pre-service and in-service programmes. This shift in focus is crucial for encouraging the development of teachers who can navigate the

complexities of real-world classrooms and communities. Firstly, teacher education programmes need to recognise that teachers do not learn in isolation but
rather within social contexts that shape their beliefs, attitudes, and practices.
Therefore, programmes should create opportunities for teachers to engage
with diverse social settings, including multilingual and multicultural environments. This can be achieved through fieldwork, internships, and collaboration •
with community partners. Secondly, when it comes to understanding curricular standards for language teaching, the emphasis should not solely be on the
logical connections between academic concepts. Instead, programmes should
encourage teachers to explore how these standards are embedded within
broader social and cultural frameworks. Highlighting social cognition in
these programmes may help teachers develop a deeper understanding of
how language teaching intersects with issues of identity, power, and social
justice. Finally, teacher education programmes should cultivate teachers'
ability to reflect on their own social locations and biases. This self-
reflexivity is essential for teachers to recognise how their own backgrounds
and experiences influence their teaching practices. Through critical reflection,
teachers can become more aware of the assumptions and values they bring into
the classroom and how these might impact students' learning experiences.
Incorporating the social dimension into teacher education practice is not only
beneficial for individual teachers but also for the broader educational system.
By preparing teachers to navigate the social complexities of teaching and
learning, we can create more inclusive and equitable classrooms that better
meet the needs of all students.

Teachers with strong social cognitive abilities are better able to understand the social and emotional needs of their students. They can identify and
address issues of inequality, diversity, and inclusion more effectively.
Additionally, they are more likely to create classroom environments that
foster positive social interactions and supportive learning communities. To
develop teachers' social cognition, teacher education programmes should
provide opportunities for teachers to engage in meaningful interactions with
diverse groups of people, including students, parents, and community mem-
bers. Furthermore, teacher education programmes should explicitly teach
social cognitive skills such as perspective-taking, empathy, and conflict
resolution. If teachers are provided with the tools to navigate social complexities, they will be better equipped to handle the challenges that arise in
real-world classrooms. Incorporating social cognition into teacher education
practice is essential for preparing teachers who are not only academically
proficient, but also socially aware and responsive to the needs of their
students.

5.2 Motivation and Emotion

Language teachers' motivation is influenced by the great variety of internal and external factors that can drive a language educator to engage in teaching activities. and seek to enhance their students' language learning (Sampson, 2016). This motivation is often fuelled by a combination of personal interests, professional goals, and a desire to make a positive impact on students' lives. On the other hand, language teachers' emotions encompass the feelings and affective states that teachers experience in their professional roles (Martínez Agudo, 2018), which can significantly influence their teaching practices and interactions with students.

A teacher's motivation and emotions are deeply intertwined with their social cognition, forming a complex system that shapes their teaching practices and interactions with students. Language teachers who possess a strong sense of motivation are often driven by a desire to foster meaningful language learning experiences among their students. This motivation is informed and influenced by the teachers' social cognition, as they draw on their understanding of social dynamics, cultural backgrounds, and learning needs to design engaging and inclusive lessons. Similarly, a teacher's emotions play a pivotal role in their teaching and are shaped by their social cognition. For example, when teachers perceive that their students are engaged and making progress in language learning, they may experience feelings of joy and accomplishment, which can further fuel their motivation to continue teaching effectively. On the other hand, if teachers sense that students are disengaged or struggling, they may feel a sense of frustration or concern. These emotions, in turn, can prompt teachers to reflect on their teaching practices and seek ways to better connect with and support their students. In essence, a teacher's social cognition provides the lens through which they view and interpret the teaching and learning process, influencing both their motivation and emotions (Shan & Xu, 2022).

As we inquire into the topic of 'motivation and emotion' in relation to language teachers' social cognition, the key approach is to focus on unpacking the complex social cognitive processes that take place within teachers' classrooms and are shaped by a multitude of factors unique to their teaching contexts. These factors may include classroom dynamics, student needs and backgrounds, cultural norms, and institutional policies. By exploring how these contextual elements interact with teachers' social cognition, we can gain a more nuanced understanding of the challenges teachers face and how they navigate them to effectively support student learning. This approach also has implications for teacher education practice, as it emphasises the need for teacher preparation programmes that are responsive to the diverse needs of learners and the complex social environments in which teaching takes place.

5.2.1 Suggestions for Future Research

Current research on language teachers' motivations and emotions has made significant progress in identifying the various factors that influence these constructs. However, there is a notable gap in our understanding of the social cognitive processes that underlie motivational and emotional change or growth among language teachers. Previous studies have predominantly focused on how motivations and emotions are triggered and developed by a range of intrinsic and extrinsic factors (e.g., Martínez Agudo, 2018; Sampson, 2016). Statistical analysis has been extensively used to validate the complex relationships between these factors and teachers' motivations and emotions. While this approach has provided valuable insights, it has often neglected the specific cognitive processes that mediate or even determine such motivational or emotional changes.

To address this gap, future research should adopt a more comprehensive framework that integrates SCT with existing models of teachers' motivations and emotions. This framework should consider how teachers' social cognitive processes, such as their ability to interpret social cues, regulate emotions, and attribute meaning to teaching experiences, influence their motivational and emotional states. By examining the intersection of social cognition, motivation, and emotion, future research may gain a deeper understanding of the dynamic nature of these constructs among language teachers. This approach could help identify the specific cognitive strategies that teachers use to manage their motivations and emotions, as well as the factors that facilitate or hinder the development of these strategies. Moreover, future research should also explore potential interventions that target social cognitive processes to enhance language teachers' motivation and emotional well-being. Such interventions could include professional development programmes that focus on building teachers' social cognitive skills, providing them with tools and strategies to more effectively navigate the social and emotional demands of teaching.

To summarise, while current research on language teachers' motivations and emotions has made valuable contributions, there is a need for a more nuanced understanding of the social cognitive processes that underlie these constructs. By adopting a comprehensive framework that integrates SCT, future research can provide crucial insights that may contribute to supporting the professional growth and well-being of language teachers.

In conclusion, current research on language teacher motivation and emotion has identified various influencing factors, yet our comprehension of the social cognitive processes behind motivational and emotional change among these teachers remains limited. Studies have predominantly focused on how motivations and emotions arise and evolve due to internal and external factors, employing statistical analyses to validate the complex relationships involved in this process. However, this approach often overlooks the cognitive processes that mediate or determine such changes. To bridge this research gap, future investigations should adopt a holistic framework that integrates SCT with existing models of teachers' motivations and emotions. This framework should consider how teachers interpret social cues, regulate their emotions, and ascribe meaning to their teaching experiences, and how these processes impact their motivational and emotional states. Exploring the intersections between social cognition, motivation, and emotion can offer deeper insights into their dynamic interplay among language teachers. Moreover, research should explore the strategies that language teachers employ to manage their motivations and emotions, along with the factors that facilitate or hinder the development of these strategies. Additionally, there is a need to investigate interventions that target social cognitive processes in order to enhance teachers' motivation and emotional well-being. Such interventions may include professional development programmes, which focus on bolstering teachers' social cognitive skills and equipping them with tools and strategies to navigate the demands of teaching more effectively.

5.2.2 Suggestions for Teacher Education Practice

The incorporation of social emotional competence and learning frameworks holds immense promise for the enhancement of language teachers' motivations and emotions in a social cognitive manner. Social emotional competence is the ability to recognise, understand, manage, and express one's own emotions, as well as to interpret and respond appropriately to the emotions of others (CASEL, 2003). Social emotional learning (SEL), on the other hand, emphasises the acquisition and application of these skills in learning and social environments (CASEL, 2012). The notion of SEL, initially outlined as 'the process by which individuals, both young and old, acquire the abilities, mindsets, and principles essential for developing social and emotional proficiency' (Elias et al., 1997, p. 2), has evolved to encompass five fundamental components of emotional proficiency among learners: self-knowledge, social understanding, self-regulation, interpersonal abilities, and prudent choice-making (CASEL, 2003; CASEL, 2012). CASEL (2003) define these elements as follows: self-knowledge involves recognising one's identity, emotions, and a realistic evaluation of personal capabilities; social understanding entails comprehending the emotions of others and effectively engaging with diverse groups; self-regulation refers to the capacity to appropriately manage one's emotions and actions; interpersonal abilities concern how an individual navigates relationships and integrates into a collective; and prudent choice-making implies the ability to make wise and accountable decisions after careful consideration of all pertinent factors.

The integration of SEL into teacher education practice is particularly relevant for language teachers, as the social and emotional demands of language teaching are unique and complex. Language teachers not only need to manage their own emotions, but must also navigate the emotional and social dynamics of their students, who are often learning a second or foreign language. By fostering social emotional competence among language teachers, teacher educators can equip them with the skills they need to create emotionally supportive and motivationally stimulating classrooms. For instance, teachers who are attuned to their own emotions and those of their students are better able to respond with empathy and understanding, which can in turn promote a sense of belonging and engagement among learners. Moreover, SEL frameworks emphasise the role of reflection and self-awareness in personal and professional growth. By encouraging language teachers to reflect on their own social and emotional experiences and practices, teacher educators can help them gain insights into how their interactions with students shape learning outcomes and motivational states. This reflective process can lead to more intentional and effective teaching practices that are responsive to the social and emotional needs of language learners.

In conclusion, the integration of social emotional competence and learning frameworks into teacher education practice offers a powerful means of promoting language teachers' motivation and emotion through social cognition. By fostering these skills among teachers, teacher educators can contribute to the creation of more inclusive, supportive, and motivating learning environments for language learners.

5.3 Resistance and Resilience

The concepts of resistance and resilience are particularly relevant to the field of language teacher development. Resistance refers here to the challenges, obstacles, and difficulties that teachers encounter in their professional growth, which can range from institutional barriers to personal insecurities (Pu & Xu, 2022). On the other hand, resilience is the capacity of teachers to adapt, overcome, and even grow from these challenges (Mansfield, 2021). It involves maintaining a positive mindset, seeking out opportunities for learning and improvement, and drawing on personal and professional resources to persevere in the face of adversity (Pooley & Cohen, 2010). Understanding these concepts is crucial for fostering a supportive environment in which language teachers can flourish and continue to develop their skills and expertise.

Language teachers operate within a complex social environment, constantly interacting with learners, colleagues, and institutional structures. Resistance, in this sense, emerges from the teachers' awareness of the social and cultural factors that can hinder their professional growth. These factors may include institutional policies that limit autonomy, cultural beliefs that undervalue teachers' work, or clashes between learners' expectations and teaching practices. Resisting these challenges requires teachers to critically reflect on their social environment, recognise oppressive structures, and seek ways to negotiate or transform them. Resilience, on the other hand, is evident in teachers' ability to draw on their social cognitive skills to adapt to and overcome these challenges. If they understand the social dynamics at play, teachers can develop strategies to cope with stress, collaborate with colleagues for support, and seek out professional development opportunities that align with their values and goals. In short, resistance and resilience are central to language teachers' social cognition because they involve an ongoing process of reflecting on, negotiating with, and adapting to the social environment in which teachers operate. By fostering these capacities, we can support the professional growth and development of language teachers.

5.3.1 Suggestions for Future Research

Our critique of current studies on teachers' resistance and resilience demonstrates that there is a predominant tendency in existing research to overemphasise teachers' agency, primarily as observed through their actions and discourses (Tao & Gao, 2021), as well as the social structure that surrounds them (Xu, 2022). While the significance of agency and structure in shaping teachers' responses to adversity should be acknowledged, this narrow focus may have led to a certain level of stagnation in the field. It has essentially established a pattern or even a 'norm' that researchers are expected to follow when approaching issues related to teachers' resistance and resilience.

However, beyond this conventional framework, there exist a plethora of alternative research foci that can shed new light on the dynamics at play. One such alternative is the study of teachers' social cognitive processes. By shifting the focus to how teachers interpret, process, and respond to social cues and information within their professional environments, we can gain deeper insights into the subtleties of their resistance and resilience. This shift in perspective promises to uncover a richer tapestry of the experiences, strategies, and challenges that teachers face, ultimately leading to a more comprehensive understanding of these phenomena. Therefore, future studies should endeavour to broaden the scope of research in this field and survey these under-explored territories. By doing so, we can move beyond the limitations of the current paradigm and towards a more holistic understanding of teachers' resistance and resilience.

For instance, language teachers' responses to forthcoming curriculum reforms can vary widely due to differences in social cognition. For instance, some teachers may strongly resist the changes because they perceive a fundamental mismatch between the key ideas underlying the reforms and their own deeply-held beliefs about language teaching. This resistance is rooted in a cognitive dissonance that arises when their personal values and the educational philosophy they endorse clash with the proposed direction of curricular reform. Other teachers who fear that they will have to undertake extra hours of training to adapt to the reforms may also express resistance, but their underlying reasons for doing so are fundamentally different. Their concern is practical and time-bound, stemming from a realistic assessment of their workload and available resources. This type of resistance is less about ideological differences and more about the logistical challenges of implementing change within an already busy schedule. If we fail to closely examine teachers' social cognition, it is easy to oversimplify their resistance as a uniform reaction to curricular reforms. Such a superficial analysis would miss the nuances of their motivations and concerns, potentially leading to ineffective or even counterproductive interventions. By contrast, a deeper understanding of teachers' social cognitions may help policymakers and administrators tailor support strategies that address the unique challenges each group faces, ultimately fostering a more positive and productive response to change.

In summary, current research on teachers' resistance and resilience tends to overemphasise teachers' agency and the surrounding social structure, creating a pattern or 'norm' that may have led the field into stagnation. To overcome this limitation, future studies should explore alternative foci, such as teachers' social cognitive processes. This shift in perspective can potentially uncover a richer tapestry of the experiences, strategies, and challenges teachers face, leading to a more comprehensive understanding of resistance and resilience. Further research is needed to examine how teachers interpret, process, and respond to social cues and information within their professional environments. By investigating these under-explored territories, we can move beyond the current paradigm's limitations and towards a more holistic understanding of resistance and resilience among language teachers.

5.3.2 Suggestions for Teacher Education Practice

Both pre-service and in-service teacher education programmes should attach greater importance to cultivating language teachers' awareness of their own and others' resistance and resilience. Teachers are often unaware that they are resisting certain aspects of their work environment, which hinders their ability to implement effective and constructive coping strategies that may help them improve the situation. By increasing their self-awareness, teachers can better identify areas of resistance, understand their underlying causes, and develop more adaptive responses. This awareness also extends to recognising resilience in themselves and their colleagues, which can foster a supportive environment where teachers can learn from each other's strengths.

Resistance and resilience may be surface phenomena that reflect more fundamental issues of social cognition. Teacher educators and school administrators need to seriously consider the underlying social cognitive processes that shape these dynamics. By exploring the beliefs, values, and perceptions that inform teachers' resistance and resilience, educators can gain a deeper understanding of the factors that influence teachers' responses to change and challenge. This knowledge will enable more targeted and effective support for teachers, helping them navigate complex social and educational landscapes.

Resistance and resilience are also intimately linked to teachers' psychological well-being and health. Therefore, these aspects should be integral components of efforts to promote teachers' health. Teacher education programmes and school administrators should prioritise the creation of environments that foster resilience and provide resources to help teachers manage resistance. This should include offering professional development opportunities that address both personal and professional growth, providing access to mental health support services, and promoting a culture of open dialogue where teachers feel safe when expressing their challenges and successes. By holistically addressing teachers' well-being, we can cultivate a more resilient and effective teaching force capable of meeting the evolving demands of the education system.

6 Towards a Social-Cognitive Perspective on Language Teacher Development

In this Element, we have investigated the complex field of social cognition, exploring its origins, development, and application to the specific context of language teaching and teacher education. We have analysed the keywords associated with social cognition, breaking down the concept into its component parts and exploring how they relate to one another. This analysis contributes to an understanding of the overall meaning and significance of social cognition.

More specifically, Section 2 focused on the theoretical framework of social cognition. It introduced key concepts and theories related to social cognition, such as social constructivism, interactive approaches, and the role of context. Section 3 delved into the complexities and challenges associated with research on social cognition, particularly in the context of language teaching. It acknowledged that the multifaceted and dynamic nature of social cognition makes it a complex phenomenon to study. Section 4 inquired into empirical research on language teachers' social cognition. It reviewed studies examining the effectiveness of social cognitive approaches in language classrooms and language teacher development, and discussed the findings and implications of these studies. This section also identified gaps in the current research and suggested areas for further exploration. Section 5 discussed potential future directions for research on language teachers' social cognition, highlighting emerging trends and issues in the field and suggesting ways of advancing the research agenda. This could include exploring new methodological approaches, examining the impact of technology on social cognitive processes in language learning, or investigating the role of social cognition in specific contexts or within specific teacher populations.

Social cognition, which encompasses the ability to understand and interpret social cues, manage interpersonal relationships, and navigate social environments, is fundamental to effective teaching and learning. However, despite its importance, language teachers' social cognition has not been recognised as an independent field of inquiry, leading to a lack of comprehensive investigation into its inherent issues, value, and potential.

By adopting a social cognitive perspective in research on language teacher education, we can gain a deeper understanding of the social and cultural factors that shape language teachers' beliefs, attitudes, and practices. This understanding can inform the design of more targeted and culturally responsive teacher education programmes that address the unique needs and challenges faced by language teachers. Such programmes can foster the development of teachers' social cognitive skills, enabling them to create inclusive and supportive learning environments that promote engagement and achievement among their students. Moreover, integrating a social cognitive perspective into the practice of language teacher education can empower teachers to reflect on their own social and cultural identities and how these identities influence their teaching. This process of self-reflection may lead to a greater awareness of the impact of social factors on language learning and motivate teachers to seek out opportunities for professional growth and development.

In summary, the social cognitive perspective offers a valuable framework for research on language teacher education and practices which aim to promote language teachers' development. By recognising and investigating the social dimensions of language teaching, we can enhance teachers' ability to navigate the complexities of the social world and foster more effective learning experiences among their students.

As we draw this Element on the exploration of language teachers' social cognition to a close, it is imperative to acknowledge the potential theoretical, methodological, and ethical complexities that accompany such an endeavour. Firstly, from a theoretical perspective, the concept of social cognition, while recognised as an independent construct in scientific research, must be viewed holistically as an integral component of teachers' learning and development. Isolating social cognition and overemphasising its role can lead to a distorted understanding of the intricate interplay between cognitive processes, emotional responses, and social interactions in the classroom.

Methodologically, exploring social cognition poses challenges related to data collection and analysis. Accessing teachers' inner cognitive landscapes and accurately interpreting their social perceptions can be a daunting task. Qualitative methods such as interviews and observations, though valuable, are subject to interpretive biases and the influence of researchers' own cognitive frameworks. Quantitative approaches, on the other hand, may struggle to capture the nuanced and context-dependent nature of social cognition.

Ethically, researchers must tread carefully to ensure that teachers' privacy and autonomy are respected. The delicate balance between gaining insights into teachers' cognitive worlds and maintaining their trust and confidentiality is paramount. Additionally, there is a need to recognise the potential power dynamics at play, particularly when research findings may have implications for teachers' professional practices and their evaluation.

In conclusion, while the exploration of language teachers' social cognition promises to enhance our understanding of teaching and learning processes, it is not without its challenges. A cautious and reflexive approach is warranted, one that situates social cognition within the broader context of teachers' professional lives and learning experiences. Only then can we truly appreciate its complexity and contributions to the field of language education.

References

Ambady, N., Bernieri, F. J., & Richeson, J. A. (2000). Toward a histology of social behavior: Judgmental accuracy from thin slices of the behavioral stream. In M. P. Zanna (Ed.), *Advances in experimental social psychology* (Vol. 32) (pp. 201–271). San Diego, CA: Academic Press.

Amodio, D. M. (2019). Social cognition 2.0: An interactive memory systems account. *Trends in Cognitive Sciences*, *23*(1), 21–33. https://doi.org/10.1016/j.tics.2018.10.002.

Bandura, A. (1989). Human agency in social cognitive theory. *American Psychologist*, *44*(9), 1175–1184. https://doi.org/10.1037/0003-066X.44.9.1175.

Bandura, A. (1997). *Self-efficacy: The exercise of control*. Stamford, CT: Worth.

Beauregard, M. (2004). *Consciousness, emotional self-regulation and the brain*. Amsterdam: John Benjamins.

Bluemke, M., Brand, R., Schweizer, G., & Kahlert, D. (2010). Exercise might be good for me, but I don't feel good about it: Do automatic associations predict exercise behavior? *Journal of Sport and Exercise Psychology*, *32*(2), 137–153. https://doi.org/10.1123/jsep.32.2.137.

Canter, D., Ioannou, M., Youngs, D., & Chungh, G. (2016). Person perception aspects of judgments of truthfulness in public appeals. *Psychiatry, Psychology and Law*, *23*(4), 547–562. https://doi.org/10.1080/13218719.2015.1081315.

Carlston, D. E., & Skowronski, J. J. (2005). Linking versus thinking: Evidence for the different associative and attributional bases of spontaneous trait transference and spontaneous trait inference. *Journal of Personality and Social Psychology*, *89*(6), 884–898. https://doi.org/10.1037/0022-3514.89.6.884.

CASEL. (2003). *Safe and sound: An educational leader's guide to evidence-based social and emotional learning (SEL) programs*. Chicago, IL: CASEL.

CASEL. (2012). *Effective social and emotional learning programs: Preschool and elementary school edition*. Chicago, IL: CASEL.

Chen, F., & Abdullah, R. (2023). Towards the contributing factors for the inconsistency between English as a Foreign Language (EFL) teachers' equity-oriented cognition and practices. *Psychology Research and Behavior Management*, *16*, 1631–1646. https://doi.org/10.2147/PRBM.S409680.

Coon, D., Mitterer, J. O., & Martini, T. S. (2021). *Introduction to psychology: Gateways to mind and behavior* (16th ed.). Boston, MA: Cengage.

Cooper, J., Blackman, S., & Keller, K. (2015). *The science of attitudes*. London: Routledge.

Creese, A., & Blackledge, A. (2015). Translanguaging and identity in educational settings. *Annual Review of Applied Linguistics*, *35*, 20–35. https://doi.org/10.1017/S0267190514000233.

Dagienė, V., Jasutė, E., & Dolgopolovas, V. (2021). Professional development of in-service teachers: Use of eye tracking for language classes, case study. *Sustainability*, *13*(22), 12504. https://doi.org/10.3390/su132212504.

Damasio, A. R. (1994). Descartes' error and the future of human life. *Scientific American*, *271*(4), 144. https://doi.org/10.1038/scientificamerican1094-144.

Day, C., & Gu, Q. (2009). Teacher emotions: Well being and effectiveness. In P. Schutz & M. Zembylas (Eds.), *Advances in teacher emotion research* (pp. 15–31). Boston, MA: Springer.

Decety, J., & Ickes, W. (Eds.). (2011). *The social neuroscience of empathy*. Cambridge, MA: The MIT Press.

Demarais, A., & White, V. (2005). *First impressions: What you don't know about how others see you*. New York: Bantam.

Donohoo, J. A. M. (2016). *Collective efficacy: How educators' beliefs impact student learning*. Los Angeles, CA: Corwin.

Eberhardt, J. L. (2020). *Biased: Uncovering the hidden prejudice that shapes what we see, think, and do*. London: Penguin.

Edge, J., & Garton, S. (2009). *From experience to knowledge in ELT*. Oxford: Oxford University Press.

Elias, M. J., Zins, J. E., Weissberg, R. P. et al. (1997). *Promoting social and emotional learning: Guidelines for educators*. Alexandria: Association for Supervision and Curriculum Development.

Fagan, D. S. (2015). When learner inquiries arise: Marking teacher cognition as it unfolds 'in-the-moment'. *Ilha Do Desterro*, *68*(1), 75–90. http://dx.doi.org/10.5007/2175-8026.2015v68n1p75.

Farrell, T. S. C. (2022). *Reflective language teaching*. Cambridge: Cambridge University Press.

Fletcher-Watson, S., Findlay, J. M., Leekam, S. R., & Benson, V. (2008). Rapid detection of person information in a naturalistic scene. *Perception*, *37*(4), 571–583. https://doi.org/10.1068/p5705.

Frith, U., & Blakemore, S. (2006). Social cognition. In R. Morris, L. Tarassenko, & M. Kenward (Eds.), *Cognitive systems – Information processing meets brain science* (pp. 138–162). Amsterdam: Elsevier.

Frith, C. D., & Frith, U. (2008). Implicit and explicit processes in social cognition. *Perspective*, *60*(3), 503–510. https://doi.org/10.1016/j.neuron.2008.10.032.

Gawronski, B., & Bodenhausen, G. V. (2006). Associative and propositional processes in evaluation: An integrative review of implicit and explicit attitude change. *Psychological Bulletin, 132*(5), 692–731. https://doi.org/ 10.1037/0033-2909.132.5.692.

Giddens, A., Duneier, M., Appelbaum, R. P., & Carr, D. (2021). *The introduction to sociology* (12th Seagull ed.). New York: W. W. Norton.

Haselton, M. G., & Funder, D. C. (2006). The evolution of accuracy and bias in social judgment. In M. Schaller, J. A. Simpson, & D. T. Kenrick (Eds.), *Evolution and social psychology* (pp. 15–37). Madison, CT: Psychosocial Press.

Herpertz, S. C., & Bertsch, K. (2014). The social-cognitive basis of personality disorders. *Current Opinion in Psychiatry, 27*(1), 73–77. https://doi.org/ 10.1097/YCO.0000000000000026.

Hinshelwood, R. D. (2023). *The mystery of emotions: Seeking a theory of what we feel*. Beijing: Phoenix Publishing House.

Hiver, P. (2017). Tracing the signature dynamics of language teacher immunity: A Retrodictive Qualitative Modeling study. *The Modern Language Journal, 101*(4), 669–690. https://doi.org/10.1111/modl.12433.

Hochschild, A. R. (2012). *The outsourced self: What happens when we pay others to live our lives for us*. New York: Metropolitan Books.

Hristov, H., Erjavec, K., Pravst, I., Juvančič, L., & Kuhar, A. (2023). Identifying differences in consumer attitudes towards local foods in organic and national voluntary quality certification schemes. *Foods, 12*(6), 1132. https://doi.org/ 10.3390/foods12061132.

Hunt, C., Borgida, E., & Lavine, H. (2012). Social cognition. In V. S. Ramachandran (Ed.), *Encyclopedia of human behaviour* (Vol. 3) (pp. 456–462). London: Academic Press.

Keltner, D., Oatley, K., & Jenkins, J. M. (2013). *Understanding emotions* (3rd ed.). Hoboken, NJ: Wiley.

Kempson, R. M. (Ed.). (1990). *Mental representations: The interface between language and reality*. Cambridge: Cambridge University Press.

Kiel, E., Heimlich, U., Markowetz, R., Braun, A., & Weiß, S. (2016). How to cope with stress in special needs education? Stress-inducing dysfunctional cognitions of teacher students: The perspective of professionalisation. *European Journal of Special Needs Education, 31*(2), 202–219. https://doi .org/10.1080/08856257.2015.1125693.

King, M. (2022). *Social chemistry: Decoding the patterns of human connection*. London: Dutton.

Kite, M. E., & Whitley, B. E. (2016). *Psychology of prejudice and discrimination* (3rd ed.). London: Routledge.

Koelkebeck, K., Uwatoko, T., Tanaka, J., & Kret, M. E. (2017). How culture shapes social cognition deficits in mental disorders: A review. *Social Neuroscience, 12*(2), 102–112. https://doi.org/10.1080/17470919.2016.1155482.

Kut, E. (2012). *Neurochemical aspects of emotional pain modulation: A multi perspective study*. Stuttgart: Südwestdeutscher Verlag für Hochschulschriften.

Lench, H. C. (2018). *The function of emotions: When and why emotions help us*. Cham: Springer.

Li, W. (2024). Transformative pedagogy for inclusion and social justice through translanguaging, co-learning, and transpositioning. *Language Teaching, 57*(2), 203–214. https://doi.org/10.1017/S0261444823000186.

Li, Z., & Xu, Y. (2021). Sustaining the effective use of materials in language classrooms: A conceptual understanding of teacher knowledge for materials use. *Sustainability, 13*(14), 8115. https://doi.org/10.3390/su13148115.

Luque-Reca, O., García-Martínez, I., Pulido-Martos, M., Burguera, J. L., & Augusto-Landa, J. M. (2022). Teachers' life satisfaction: A structural equation model analyzing the role of trait emotion regulation, intrinsic job satisfaction and affect. *Teaching and Teacher Education, 113*, 103668. https://doi.org/10.1016/j.tate.2022.103668.

Maio, G. R., Verplanken, B., & Haddock, G. (2018). *The psychology of attitudes and attitude change* (3rd ed.). Guildford: Sage.

Mansfield, C. F. (Ed.). (2021). *Cultivating teacher resilience: International approaches, applications and impact*. Singapore: Springer.

Martínez Agudo, J. D. D. (Ed.). (2018). *Emotions in second language teaching: Theory, research and teacher education*. New York: Springer.

McBride, D. M., & Cutting, J. C. (2018). *Cognitive psychology: Theory, process, and methodology*. Guildford: Sage.

Moscovici, S. (2000). *Social representations: Explorations in social psychology*. Cambridge, MA: Polity Press.

Moskowitz, G. B. (2005). *Social cognition: Understanding self and others*. New York: The Guilford Press.

Nadler, J. T., & Voyles, E. C. (Eds.). (2020). *Stereotypes: The incidence and impacts of bias*. Santa Barbara, CA: Praeger.

Niedenthal, P. M., & Ric, F. (2017). *Psychology of emotion* (2nd ed.). London: Routledge.

Poh, S. K. (2021). English language teachers' appropriation of tools in the Singapore classrooms: A socio-cultural analysis. *Asia Pacific Journal of Education, 41*(4), 740–753. https://doi.org/10.1080/02188791.2021.1997706.

Pooley, J. A., & Cohen, L. (2010). Resilience: A definition in context. *The Australian Community Psychologist, 22*(1), 30–37.

Priest, H. (2019). *Biases and heuristics: The complete collection of cognitive biases and heuristics that impair decisions in banking, finance and everything else*. Independently published.

Pu, S., & Xu, H. (2022). Resistance and agency in second language academic discourse socialisation: Undergraduate students' experiences of an EAP course. *Journal of English for Academic Purposes, 58*, 101122. https://doi.org/10.1016/j.jeap.2022.101122.

Pugh, S. D. (2001). Service with a smile: Emotional contagion in the service encounter. *Academy of Management Journal, 44*(5), 1018–1027. https://doi.org/10.5465/3069445.

Purper, C. J., Thai, Y., Frederick, T. V., & Farris, S. (2023). Exploring the challenge of teachers' emotional labor in early childhood settings. *Early Childhood Education Journal, 51*, 781–789. https://doi.org/10.1007/s10643-022-01345-y.

Rahimi, M., & Ong, K. K. W. (2023). Exploring expert teachers' cognitions and practices of teaching English speaking and their students' experiences and engagement. *System, 115*, 103064. https://doi.org/10.1016/j.system.2023.103064.

Randolph, P. (2016). *The psychology of conflict: Mediating in a diverse world*. London: Bloomsbury Continuum.

Reeves, J. R. (2006). Secondary teacher attitudes toward including English-Language Learners in mainstream classrooms. *The Journal of Educational Research, 99*(3), 131–143. https://doi.org/10.3200/JOER.99.3.131-143.

Sampson, R. (2016). EFL teacher motivation in-situ: Co-adaptive processes, openness and relational motivation over interacting timescales. *Studies in Second Language Learning and Teaching, 6*(2), 293–318. http://dx.doi.org/10.14746/ssllt.2016.6.2.6.

Sarab, M. R. A., & Mardian, F. (2023). Reflective practice in second language teacher education: A scoping review. *Journal of Education for Teaching, 49*(5), 768–784. https://doi.org/10.1080/02607476.2022.2152316.

Schwarzenthal, M., Daumiller, M., & Civitillo, S. (2023). Investigating the sources of teacher intercultural self-efficacy: A three-level study using TALIS 2018. *Teaching and Teacher Education, 126*, 104070. https://doi.org/10.1016/j.tate.2023.104070.

Sercu, L., Bandura, E., Castro, P. et ale. (2005). *Foreign language teachers and intercultural competence: An international investigation*. Bristol: Multilingual Matters.

Shan, Z., & Xu, H. (2022). Exploring multilingual awareness development in learners of multiple foreign languages: A social cognitive perspective. *Journal of Multilingual and Multicultural Development*. (online first) https://doi.org/10.1080/01434632.2022.2092119.

Shan, Z., & Xu, H. (2023). Teacher beliefs about teaching French as a foreign language in a Chinese university: A multilingual perspective. *Porta Linguarum*, (VIII), 169–182. https://doi.org/10.30827/portalin.viVIII.29247.

Smith E. R., & DeCoster, J. (2000). Dual-process models in social and cognitive psychology: Conceptual integration and links to underlying memory systems. *Personality and Social Psychology Review*, *4*(2), 108–131. https://doi.org/10.1207/S15327957PSPR0402_01.

Sun, C., Wei, L., & Young, R. F. (2022). Measuring teacher cognition: Comparing Chinese EFL teachers' implicit and explicit attitudes toward English language teaching methods. *Language Teaching Research*, *26*(3), 382–410. https://doi.org/10.1177/1362168820903010.

Sutherland, C. A. M., Young, A. W., & Rhodes, G. (2017). Facial first impressions from another angle: How social judgements are influenced by changeable and invariant facial properties. *British Journal of Psychology*, *108*(2), 397–415. https://doi.org/10.1111/bjop.12206.

Tao, J., & Gao, X. (2021). *Language teacher agency*. Cambridge: Cambridge University Press.

Urzúa, A., & Asención-Delaney, Y. (2023). Examining novice language teachers' reflections in an online community of practice. *Foreign Language Annals*, *56*(1), 53–74. https://doi.org/10.1111/flan.12672.

Van Rheenen, T. E., Meyer, D., & Rossell, S. L. (2014). Pathways between neurocognition, social cognition and emotion regulation in bipolar disorder. *Acta Psychiatrica Scandinavica*, *130*(5), 397–405. https://doi.org/10.1111/acps.12295.

Vidergor, H. E. (2023). The effect of teachers' self-innovativeness on accountability, distance learning self-efficacy, and teaching practices. *Computers and Education*, *199*, 104777. https://doi.org/10.1016/j.compedu.2023.104777.

Wang, H., & Hall, N. C. (2021). Exploring relations between teacher emotions, coping strategies, and intentions to quit: A longitudinal analysis. *Journal of School Psychology*, *86*, 64–77. https://doi.org/10.1016/j.jsp.2021.03.005.

Wang, J., Lan, J. Y., Khairutdinova, R. R., & Gromova, C. R. (2022). Teachers' attitudes to cultural diversity: Results from a qualitative study in Russia and Taiwan. *Frontiers in Psychology*, *13*, 976659. https://doi.org/10.3389/fpsyg.2022.976659.

Wharton, A. S. (2009). The sociology of emotional labor. *Annual Review of Sociology*, *35*, 147–165. https://doi.org/10.1146/annurev-soc-070308-115944.

Wyatt, M. (2016). "Are they becoming more reflective and/or efficacious?" A conceptual model mapping how teachers' self-efficacy beliefs might grow. *Educational Review*, *68*(1), 114–137. https://doi.org/10.1080/00131911.2015.1058754.

Xu, H. (2013). From the imagined to the practiced: A case study on novice EFL teachers' professional identity change in China. *Teaching and Teacher Education, 31*, 79–86. http://dx.doi.org/10.1016/j.tate.2013.01.006.

Xu, H. (2015). Developing novice EFL teachers' pedagogical knowledge through lesson study activities. In T. S. C. Farrell (Ed.), *International perspectives on language teacher education: Innovations from the field* (pp. 181–192). Basingstoke: Palgrave Macmillan.

Xu, H. (2019). Putonghua as "admission ticket" to linguistic market in minority regions in China. *Language Policy, 18*(1), 17–37. https://doi.org/10.1007/s10993-018-9462-x.

Xu, H. (2022). Open access publishing and university researchers' agency towards reshaping the publishing habitus. *Education as Change, 26*, 11390. https://doi.org/10.25159/1947-9417/11390.

Yin, M. (2010). Understanding classroom language assessment through teacher thinking research. *Language Assessment Quarterly, 7*(2), 175–194. https://doi.org/10.1080/15434300903447736.

Yuan, R., Lee, I., Xu, H., & Zhang, H. (2023). The alchemy of teacher mindfulness: Voices from veteran language teachers in China. *Professional Development in Education, 49*(2), 323–339. https://doi.org/10.1080/19415257.2020.1814383.

Zheng, H. (2015). *Teacher beliefs as a complex system: English language teachers in China*. New York: Springer.

Cambridge Elements ⹄

Critical Issues in Teacher Education

Tony Loughland
University of New South Wales

Tony Loughland is an Associate Professor in the School of Education at the University of New South Wales, Australia. Tony is currently leading projects on using AI for citizens' informed participation in urban development, the provision of staffing for rural and remote areas in NSW and on Graduate Ready Schools.

Andy Gao
University of New South Wales

Andy Gao is a Professor in the School of Education at the University of New South Wales, Australia. He edits various internationally-renowned journals, such as International Review of Applied Linguistics in Language Teaching for De Gruyter and Asia Pacific Education Researcher for Springer.

Hoa T. M. Nguyen
University of New South Wales

Hoa T. M. Nguyen is an Associate Professor in the School of Education at the University of New South Wales, Australia. She specializes in teacher education/development, mentoring and sociocultural theory.

About the Series

This series addresses the critical issues teacher educators and teachers are engaged with in the increasingly complex profession of teaching. These issues reside in teachers' response to broader social, cultural and political shifts and the need for teachers' professional education to equip them to teach culturally and linguistically diverse students.

Cambridge Elements $^{\equiv}$

Critical Issues in Teacher Education

Elements in the Series

A full series listing is available at: www.cambridge.org/EITE